To Kristin

S ound has a profound effect on the senses. It can be both heard and felt. It can even be seen with the mind's eye. It can almost be tasted and smelled. Sound can evoke responses of the five senses. Sound can paint a picture, produce a mood, trigger the senses to remember another time and place. From infancy we hear sound with our entire bodies. When I hear my own name, I have as much a sense of it entering my body through my back or my hand or my chest as through my ears. Sound speaks to the sensorium; the entire system of nerves that stimulates sensual response.

Table of Contents

Author's Note to the British Reader

This book can be used by actors in the U.S., the U.K., or any part of the English-speaking world. Although some examples of phonetic transcription are given in my native accent—New Jersey, U.S.—this is done to stress the importance of working from one's own accent and not following the strictures of an imposed standard accent. The process outlined in this book is a springboard into a profound understanding of the way you yourself speak, and the application of this understanding into the crafting of character accents.

Throughout this book, British and American accents are compared. You will, therefore, work with sounds that occur naturally in your own accent as well as with sounds that are foreign to you. In Part One, Phonetic Pillows, you will be introduced to each phonetic symbol and the sound it represents. For the purposes of Part One, it is important that you identify these symbols with the sounds of your own accent. Slight modification of the symbols may be necessary to accurately represent the way you speak. As a general guideline for such modification, see the "Comparison of British, U.S., and 'Good Speech for Classic Texts'" on page 112.

Acknowledgments

I lovingly thank my whole family for their encouragement, support and editorial advice throughout this project, my parents Pat and Jim Colaianni, and my brothers and sisters Karen, Janice, James and John; and Pam who is always with me. Thanks also to my sister-in-law, Lila. Thanks to my colleagues at the University of Missouri in Kansas City who have in one way or another helped move this book on to completion, Dale AJ Rose, Joseph Appelt, Jennifer Martin, Theodore Swetz, Felicia Londre, Mary Guaraldi and Vincent Scassalatti. Thank you to Howard Martin for information on segmental analysis. Thanks also to Gayla Voss and the costume shop of the Missouri Repertory Theater for making the first set of phonetic pillows. To Lisa Thompson and Kathy Hirner for doing the actual cutting and sewing. To George Keathley, Artistic Director of Missouri Rep for giving me a place to put my work into practice. To my teacher Tina Packer whose influence I strongly feel in these pages. To the entire faculty of Shakespeare & Company for their support and encouragement. Thank you to Claudia Anderson for many hours of consultation during the preparation of this book. Thanks to the many teachers around the country using this approach for their generous feedback and suggestions, especially: Christine Adaire, De Paul University; Claudia Anderson, California Institute for the Arts; Judy Shahn, University of Washington, Seattle; Walton Wilson, Southern Methodist University; Jim Daniels, University of Michigan, Kalamazoo; Mary Coy, University of Virginia; Timothy Douglas, Denver Theater Center; Joe Gilday, Iowa State University; Ruth Rootburg, University of Illinois. Thanks to Jean Wilson, Zeb Hodge and Kathy Scherer for their help in preparing the manuscript. To Sara Barker for her wisdom and guidance. To Quentin Crisp for sharing with me his observations about acting, teaching and writing. To my friends Andrea Haring, Larry Nathanson, Michaela Murphy, Julie Nelson, Normi Noel, Fran Bennet, Tess Brubeck, and Faith Barlow for feedback on early drafts. To Ralph Pine, editor-in-chief of Drama Book Publishers for his vision of what actor-training can be and for his faith in me and my work. And most especially to my editor Judith Durant for countless hours of detailed, painstaking labor throughout the many phases of this project. Thanks to Brenda Mason for continuing to build phonetic pillows for teachers and institutions around the country. To Linda Amayo and Douglas Stewart for teaching phonetics in this way as my assistants at UMKC. Thank you to the MFA Acting class of 1993 at UMKC for helping me to develop the games described in this book: Kimberly Martin-Cotten, Mike Larson, Bill Harper, Jonathan Wade, Rachelle Eves, David Solovieff and Richard Mahar. Thanks to George Mount for his sketches which served as the model for the illustrations in this book. Thanks to Sue Griffith who gave me my first opportunity to teach phonetics in higher education, and to Judy Matsunobu for letting me teach pronunciation in her wonderful ESL program. Thanks to Robert Leibacher and Glenne Bruce of the Boston Conservatory who introduced me to phonetics. Finally it is with love and awe that I acknowledge Kristin Linklater whose work with Sound & Movement inspires me to bring Life and Humanity to this thing they call "speech."

Louis Colaianni
Kansas City, 1994

Introduction

A *fun* approach to phonetics? Is this a contradiction in terms? Graduates of actor training programs often remember the tedium and dullness of a phonetics course long after they have forgotten the phonetic symbols themselves. Phonetics can be a wonderful way to explore the sounds of language and develop individual expressiveness. Unfortunately, the goal of most phonetic courses is "accent correction." In these courses students have an artificially engineered "standard" accent foisted on them. Phonetics as taught in actor training programs often has the feeling of an academic rather than a performance class. Success can be measured by right answers—correct pronunciations. Unlike Voice, Movement, and Acting classes, the Phonetics class may lack a direct connection to creative impulse. There is, however, a way to involve the right brain (and the body) as well as the left brain in the learning of phonetics. This process, in combination with voice-freeing exercises, can eliminate the need for teaching Standard Speech in the usual sense.

I've been inspired by the ideas of inventive phonetics teachers who have their students run phonetic relay races, play phonetic hop-scotch, etc. I find that by gearing my phonetic class toward the physicality of other performance classes, actors retain the symbols better and use them more creatively in their study of stage accents. In combination with the voice work that I teach, phonetics actually helps to open and develop the actors's voices. I don't teach standard speech— explorations with phonetics help my students find maximum intelligibility, openness, and vocal freedom. They lose the limitations of regionalisms without having the life's blood of individuality drained from their voices.

Exploring phonetics becomes a way of grounding the voice in the body, fully experiencing the sensuality of language, and developing relaxed, open sound.

This approach to phonetics and accents replaces marks on a chalkboard with throwable, huggable phonetic symbol-shaped pillows. In cooperation with your imagination, these sound-endowed pillows will activate your voice and all your body parts into expression. With these pillows you can scramble and unscramble the entire language. This work is very physical and playing with the pillows will teach you how to read and write phonetically.

A very lively exploration of contrasting sounds can also convince your whole being to communicate honestly and sincerely in any accent.

The pillows I use with my students were built by the Missouri Repertory Theatre costume shop. The material used was scrap from productions. The artists who designed them decided what textures and patterns went with each sound. They're each about a foot square and weigh about a half a pound, though even the size and weight varies a little for big or little sounds.

There are pillows of linen, silk, satin, wool, cotton—all sorts of textures. There are red, green, black, blue, pink, orange, purple, yellow, and white pillows. There are pillows in all sorts of patterns—polka dots, plaids, floral prints, stripes, and solids.

Pillows are great for this work. After all, pillows are sensual. We sleep with pillows. They mold to the body.

The pillows are weighted so that you can tell the bottom from the top. They are all backed in the same solid color so you can distinguish front from back.

Although pillows work great, you can substitute other objects. If you don't mind giving up the shapes, textures, and weights, you can draw each symbol on a balloon. If you want something more bouncy and throwable, try rubber balls. You could even cut the symbols out of double sheets of construction paper, stuff them with cotton, and glue them together. There are probably a hundred substitutions. Be inventive. To do this work at all, you need to be inventive.

Below is one teacher's account of getting started with the phonetic pillows:

Dear Teacher:

In August 1992, I attended a workshop presented by Louis Colaianni at the ATHE National Conference held in Atlanta. After accepting a position to teach Voice and Diction, I thought an alternative method of presenting IPA would supplement my approach. It was only after the "Flinging Pillows" workshop that I realized what Colaianni terms the true "joy of phonetics."

When I began that fall quarter, I did not have a set of phoneme-shaped pillows, so in my first class I offered extra credit to any students willing to help create them. Working periodically over the next couple of months, two students and I began creating the three-dimensional phonemes from butcher-paper patterns. We used bowls and paint cans to make various sized circles, and, of course, a 12-inch straight edge rule for straight lines. We then dug through some old, leftover material in the theatre department to find enough different scraps to make the fronts of the pillows. The back of each pillow was then cut of cheap, white muslin, also excess.

I explored many ideas in regard to a stuffing method that would indicate the difference between the top and the bottom of the pillow. I finally settled on a black line and downward pointing arrow on the back side of each to indicate the bottom. The phonemes are thus machine washable and should last for some time. Since I found scrap material, my only expense was the stuffing (some of which I found backstage, also.)

In the winter term, I was finally able to put my pillows into use. In practice, the playfulness of the flinging pillows energized the class and, simply put, we had a ball! I have combined the flinging pillows with chalk marks on a blackboard to teach IPA with favorable results. Quiz grades were consistently higher than in the past.

This is the future of teaching IPA. The visceral approach is not only fun, but it also aids in student retention of material taught. It can go as far as the creativity of the students and instructor wish to take it. While learning, all can truly experience "The Joy of Phonetics."

Sincerely yours,

Patrick Gagliano, Instructor
Department of Visual and Performing Arts
Central Piedmont Community College
Charlotte, North Carolina

Here is the International Phonetic Alphabet:

ɪ ɪ e ɛ æ a ɑ ə ɚ ʌ ɝ ɜ ɒ ɔ o ʊ u aɪ ɔɪ aʊ

oʊ eɪ ju b p g kd t v f h ʤ j l m n r s

ʃ w ð θ z ʒ ŋ ʧ hw

As you can see, it's very much like the alphabet that we use every day but with certain strange new symbols. Since Elizabethan times many different phonetic systems have been developed for a variety of purposes such as spelling reform, standardizing pronunciation, teaching deaf people to speak, and studying accents and dialects. In fact, the present day IPA isn't very different from the "alphabet of regular orthography" set down by Thomas Smith in the 1500s.

If the IPA looks like Greek to you, imagine learning the "Visible Speech" alphabet invented by Alexander Melville Bell (the telephone-inventor's father) in the 1860s:

Or the phonetic characters John Wilkins used in 1668 to transcribe "The Lord's Prayer":

3

The IPA is certainly less complicated than either of these, but still people have trouble learning and remembering it. Whatever your experience with phonetics and dialects has been, you probably haven't gone this route before.

Working with phonetics can be dull. My teacher once said that phonetics was invented in order to "murder language and close the book on it once and for all."

Let's take a second look at these phonetic symbols, not as dead language on the page, but as the elements of language that live and breathe in all of us.

i ɪ eɪ ɜ ɛ æ ɑ ɒ ə

ʌ ɚ ɝ ɔ oʊ ʊ u ɑɪ ɔɪ

aʊ ju j ɔ æ e

b k d f g h hw ʤ l

m n p r s ʃ tʃ ð θ

v w z ʒ ŋ tʃ

The first thing you need to do is to breathe life into these phonetic symbols. You've got to get them off the page and touch them. Let them touch you, too. Let them touch every part of your body just as sound waves do. Rather than beginning this process with drills and blackboard transcription, dump out all of your phonetic symbols in front of you. Feel them in your hands. Mix them into a language soup. You can't do this with a blackboard.

The exploration that follows can be done solo, or in a group. After you've done the exercise, the directions and illustrations will serve as a reference for the phonetic symbols and their sounds.

If you're working with a group, be aware that there is a range of differences in the way people form the same sound. Even among people who share a national accent, there may be two or more versions of the same sound. For now don't worry about uniformity, it's perfectly natural that people of varied backgrounds will form sounds slightly differently—particularly vowel sounds.

Vowels

To begin, fish through the pile for the /u / shaped pillow and reel it in.

The phonetic symbols in this book will be distinguished from Roman alphabet characters by being placed within slash marks /   / .

/u / is the symbol for the vowel sound in the words TRUE, YOU, CLUE, THROUGH, BROOD. Here is a line from scene / u / of *The Undiapered Filefish* (the play you will be working with in the back of the book):

> "It is TRUE, then, that YOU'VE been watching CLUE after
> CLUE come bristling THROUGH the fog of language, and now
> the road is almost fully behind YOU. Don't BROOD."

Say this line. Indulge the /u/. Notice how /u / feels in your mouth as you say it.

Now take the /u / pillow in your hands. Feel its weight and texture. See its shape and color. Endow this pillow with the energy and vibration of the sound /u/. Touch this pillow to your body and imagine that as it touches you, it activates your voice. Let /u/ vibrations release not only through your mouth, but through your body as well. Move the pillow over all the surfaces of your body and feel sound flowing from the inside of your torso, arms, legs, head, feet, out into the air. Let your body be moved by the sound that flows through it. Imagine that sound vibrations actually caused movement. Notice how different parts of your body respond to the sound. As /u/ moves through you what images (colors, for instance) and feelings (happy, sad, angry, etc.) come up for you?

Once you are completely satisfied that your whole body and all its parts have had an experience of this sound, drop the pillow creating a second pile for sounds you've already worked with. Now pick up the /ɑ/ pillow. / ɑ/ is the easily recognizable symbol for the vowel sound in SPA and FATHER.

Here is a line from scene /ɑ / of *The Undiapered Filefish*.

"I did SPA work at the PLAZA and found myself among the SUAVEST FATHERS in town."

Say this line and get the feel of /ɑ/.

Now go through the steps you followed with the /u/ pillow. Begin fresh without preconceptions. Find out how /ɑ/ activates your body and voice in a different way. If you began by rubbing /u/ on your knees, begin applying this sound to a completely different part of your body. Continue letting /ɑ/ activate your voice and body parts until you feel completely satisfied with the exploration. Notice how /ɑ/ feels in your body. How do the images and feelings that come up differ from those that came up with /u/?

Continue as above with the other pillows until you have gone through all of the sounds. Follow the same steps you went through with /u/ and /ɑ/. For each sound you will have a line from *The Undiapered Filefish*. Say the line, indulging that sound. Feel the sound in your mouth. Pick up the pillow. Feel it, see it. Rub the pillow over your body. Feel the sound moving through your body. Stay loose and relaxed. If you find you're holding part of your body in a fixed position, let it go. Let the sound move your body. Don't move first and then add sound. You can't plan what's going to happen. Let the sound surprise you. Notice how the sound affects you physically, emotionally, imaginatively. Continue working with each pillow until you have thoroughly explored the possibilities of that sound traveling through your body.

"Where's my GOOD COOK hiding her SUGAR supplies?"

This sound is different from the first two you played with. It's shorter in duration; it needs to repeat more often. As you continue, notice which sounds are inherently short, inherently long, and which ones are somewhere in between.

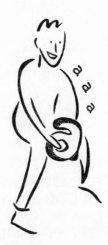

"I RANG the LAD AND he used LAN-
GUAGE AS though it were AN AX."

"I'd RATHER BASK in the PATH of my
PASTOR than fight a RAFT of NASTY
bowls of chowder."

If /æ / and /a / seem to have the identical sound, that's OK for now. We'll deal with them more specifically later. Take a minute to compare the two lines from the play. Notice if there is any subtle difference between the two sounds as you read the lines. Then go back to playing with the /a / pillow with any new awareness you may have.

"They BOUGHT the bit of WALL at the AUCTION."

"WHAT COMEDY this NOD to the POSSIBLE INVOLVEMENT
OF GOD is the religion OF the ODD COLLEGE SCHOLAR."

If this sound seems identical to /ɑ / ("I did SPA work in the PLAZA..."), that's
OK for now. But, as above with /æ / and /ɑ / , say the /ɒ / and /ɑ / lines from the
play and notice any differences. Then use any new awareness as you play with the
/ɒ / pillow. (For more information on /ɑ / and /ɒ / see page 36.)

"I do not AGREE with the ACCOUNT of the ATTACK."
(This is a little sound.)

If this sound seems the same as /ə / that's because it is. It's the same *sound* but in the *accented*
part of a word. /ə / is an *un*accented sound.

"A MUG of MUD pie LOVE JUST for you."

"Shall I GET the NET? I could put TOGETHER a KETTLE of THEM by FEBRUARY."

"I'm HIP to the GLIB gab of BEING by the MILL, but WILL the CHIN CONVINCE?"

"Might WE BELIEVE they are both in NEED of a LEADER?"

When you've completely finished with / i / throw it onto the discard pile and then get into the pile yourself. Move through the pile; let not just your hands but all parts of your body come in contact with different sound pillows. As you randomly encounter each pillow, let its sound release through and move whatever part of your body it touches. Let sounds begin to run together and form other more complex sounds. Let one long stream of sound release through your body—constantly changed by the influence of whatever sound pillow you happen to meet.

Discover all the different ways these sounds can combine.

Some of these combinations will feel very familiar to you because you use them in words all the time. Other combinations never come up in English words at all, and present brand new possibilities for expressing ideas and feelings.

Now that you've combined these sounds in all different ways, let's look at some of the combinations we use in everyday speaking. First pick up the / ɔ / pillow and run its sound through your body a few times. Next switch to the / ɪ / pillow and let it release through your body many times. Now take both pillows and combine them. Let them blend into a new sound that starts with / ɔ / and ends with / ɪ / .

You will end up with something like the / ɔɪ / sound in CHOICE, SPOIL, BOY. Here's a line from scene / ɔɪ / in *The Undiapered Filefish*:

"You've got no CHOICE.
Either SPOIL the BOY or
make him a LOYAL man."

Say the line, indulge the / ɔɪ / . Feel the sound in your mouth. Now find the / ɔɪ / pillow and let its sound invade your body. Move in the ways / ɔɪ / wants you to move. Express whatever / ɔɪ / wants to express through you. Continue until you have completely exhausted the possibilities of / ɔɪ / .

Find the / a / pillow, keep the / ɪ / pillow nearby. As above, begin working with / a / and / ɪ / separately. Then combine them into a sound that begins with / a / and ends in / ɪ / . The new sound you have created will be something like the vowel sound in FIND, SLIME, BRIBE, BRINE, SPY and TIGHT.

Say this line from the play:

> "He's helped us FIND and nab the SLIME taking a BRIBE. He worked with a group of BRINE to bring down the SPY ring in TIGHT pants."

Notice how the / aɪ /s feel. Now find the / aɪ / pillow and send its sound through your body. Continue until your hunger for / aɪ / has been sated.

Find the / a / pillow and the / ʊ / pillow. First, play with them separately; then combine them into a single sound that begins with / a / and ends with / ʊ / . You will end up with a sound similar to the vowel in HOW, COW, HOUSE.

Say this line several times:

> "HOW can a COW ROUSE a hen HOUSE?"

Try any other / aʊ / words you can think of.

Then get the / aʊ / pillow and let its sound fill you and move you.

Pick up the / o / pillow. This is the / o / sound in OBEY and DOMAIN. Notice that in these words the / o / appears in the unstressed syllables. (More about this later.) Let / o / release its sound through your body many times.

Now find the / ʊ / pillow and combine it with the / o / pillow. Let the two sounds blend into a new sound that starts with / o / and ends with / ʊ /. You'll end up with / oʊ /. This sound is very much like / o / but it's longer and more powerful. It gets more stress in words.

Throw / o / and / ʊ / back on the pile and find the / oʊ / pillow. Let / oʊ / vibrations move your body.

"I KNOW you want a LOAD of OATS to make that GROTESQUE OKRA pound cake."

Find the / e / pillow. This is the vowel in the words PLAY, GAIN, FADE. However, all by itself it's very short. Let this short little sound move through your body.

The way this sound is generally used in the English language, it needs a little boost to make it longer. Find the /ɪ / pillow and combine it with an /e / . Let the sound begin with /e / and end with / ɪ / . You'll end up with /eɪ/ as in this line from the play:

"It could be our GAIN if the PLAY FADES."

Throw / e / and / ɪ / back on the pile and pick up / eɪ / . Move /eɪ / through your body. Let its vibrations move you.

Before going on to the next batch of sounds, play with these pillows as much as you like in order to get your body sensitized and responsive to their vibrations.

The more you play with them, the better you will remember the symbol for each sound.

Consonants

Notice that throughout all of the sounds that we have discussed so far, your lips always remain apart. In the next batch of sounds there is a lot of variety in what the mouth does. For some of these sounds the lips come together. Sometimes the top front teeth and the lower lip are used. At other times the top front teeth and the tip of the tongue make contact, or the tip of the tongue meets the gum ridge behind the top teeth. The soft palate and the back of the tongue will get together at some points. For some sounds the lips are relaxed and apart. Sometimes they protrude; sometimes they spring apart. Some of the sounds use the vibrations of your voice; others use just breath. As you play with these sounds let all the energy, vibration, and variety in your mouth transform into energy, vibration, and varieties of movement in your body. Some of the symbols will be very familiar to you; others you may never have encountered before. Start with the / m / pillow. This is the same "m" you use all the time as in the word ME.

Notice that your lips are lightly closed. Feel the vibrations gathering on your lips and then gathering and congregating in all the parts of the body to which you send the pillow. Continue until your whole body has felt the /m/. Let it wake up your appetite. How does /m/ taste? How do you feel?

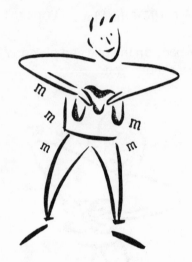

Now say this line from *Disciplining Dimes* (the CONSONANT play in the back of the book).

"That SPASM in the heart of MY BOSOM caused ME to drop
those DIMES."

Continue exploring the rest of the consonants in the same way you explored the vowels; say the line, indulge its sounds, pick up the pillow and explore its sound through your body.

When you're finished with /m/, find the /ð/ shaped pillow. This is the "th" sound in words like THAT and THE. As with the other sounds experience /ð/ with your whole body. Let the vibrations of your voice move your body.

"ALTHOUGH we feel THE two are SMOTHER-
ING one ANOTHER, BOTHER not THE delineation THUSLY."

Now switch to the / θ / shaped pillow. This is TH as in THIN or ETHER. As you play with this pillow notice that there is no voice in this sound at all; it's all breath. Let the breath move your body as you release this sound.

"We must BOTH take our OATH while we walk a SOUTH-facing PATH."

Next find the /d / pillow. As you already know, this is the quick little sound in words like DO and ADD. Touch this pillow to many, many parts of your body and let it release its vibrations many, many times.

"I'm PLEASED to report that the DATE can be TODAY LODGED in the DEED as a CONDUIT to ORDER the DATA."

After that, find the /ʒ / pillow. This is the "s" in MEASURE and the "z" in AZURE, and the "g" sound in BEIGE. As with the other sounds, send /ʒ / through your body.

"...a CASUAL affair but a VISION of great joy."

Now combine /d / and / ʒ / with the / d / as the first part of the sound and the / ʒ / as the second part. Let these two pillows play your body becoming something like the / ʤ / sound in JOE. Toss / d / and / ʒ / back into the pile and find the /ʤ / pillow. Let the / ʤ / pillow have the run of your body releasing its sound many times.

"Or should we try the GYPSY blueJAY, in GENTLE JAW in-
fused gravy?"

Now combine two other sounds:
Begin with the /t / pillow as in TO. There's no voice in this one—just breath. Get it going through your body. Let its fast little sound repeat many, many times.

"ACT natural as though THAT FATSO TWERP WEREN'T such a SOFT SIFTER."

Next find the / ʃ / pillow. This sound can be short or long and snakey like its pillow. It's the "sh" sound in SHOUT and the "t" sound in ACTION. Snake the / ʃ / pillow over your whole body as you release its sound.

"The OFFSHOOT is that SHE can SHAKE the OCEAN FISSURE with her TISSUE MACHINE."

Now, using both pillows, combine these two sounds into a new sound that begins with / t / and ends in / ʃ / .

Together they form something like "ch" in CHERRY or "t" in MATURE. Throw / t / and / ʃ / back on the pile and find the / tʃ / pillow. Move it around your body—release its sound—all breath, no voice—many times.

"I've been playing CHESS with that dime all week and it would CHOOSE to CHEAT at every turn."

Find the / h / pillow, the symbol for the sound in HOW, WHO, and HEAVY and let it sigh / h / over your whole body.

"HE HIT me! I HATE this dime."

Take the / w / pillow as in the word WE. This is a quick little sound and lip movement. Let the energy of this sound and lip-wiggle move through your body.

WE seem to WANT to DWINDLE the SWIM BETWEEN trains."

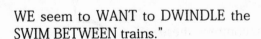

Now put the /h / and / w / together and let their sounds combine. Only this time let the /w / be voiceless, like the /h /. You'll end up with something like an /h / with a /w / movement of the lips occurring at the same time. This is the sound in WHAT, WHEN, and WHERE. Toss /h / and /w / back on the pile. Pick up the / hw /. Release its sound, and let it move your body.

"WHAT is behind the WHITENESS of a WHALE?"

Find the / j / pillow. This is the y sound of YES. Use this pillow to explore the sound on its own for awhile.

"YOU have to stop feeding the YAK the JUNGIAN dough-nuts."

Go back to your pile of vowels and find / u / . Combine / j / and / u / . They'll make something like the word "you."

Trade in the two pillows for the / ju / pillow. In some accents, this is the sound not only of YOU and CUTE but also of NEW, STUPID, and DUKE.

You might not be used to pronouncing some of these words with the / ju / sound. You might be in the habit of using plain old / u / when you say a word like DUKE. Try this passage from *The Undiapered Filefish* using / ju / instead of / u / . Get the feel of / ju / in your mouth.

The NUDE TUNA is droning on, a TUNE I ASSUMED you
KNEW DUE to the FEW LUMINESCENT RETINUES left in this
area.

Get very physical with the / ju / pillow. Convince your body that / ju / is possible—even in words you've always said as / u / .

Pick up the / ŋ / pillow. This is an "n" with the tail of a "g" and is the "ng" sound in BRING, DANCING, and SINGER. Gather the / ŋ / vibrations between your soft palate and back of tongue and let them travel through your body.

"SING to me Briggs, stop BANGING the GONG."

The rest of the symbols are very familiar. You use them all the time to read and write. They're all lower case letters so L looks like a straight line /l / rather than a right angle. Otherwise there's nothing to confuse you.

As with the other pillows, run these around your body and release their sounds.

"I'LL LOCK your desk,
I'LL LAY down the LAW."

"I feel ENLIVENED by
VIVID being INVINCIBLE."

"NAT says you're NOTHING
but a DANDY, a DUNCE, but
I like the way you DANCE."

"What do you SAY, shall
we get SOME SAKI?"

"WHOSE snappy BANGS
of ZEAL would provide
the right cover for SISTER'S
SPASMS?"

"My FATHER LEFT it
FULL ENOUGH"

"Oh BOY! What's it going to
BE, BROWN BROILED lamb
BLENDED with HERBS?"

"They ARGUE a GOOD
GARGLE, but any GUY
worth his GREEN hair
would not GET BOGGED
down in GAB about dimes."

"We PAY the bill with a PET canary
or PAT the final bilge with PAPA-like
fondness."

"They ATTACK theNUCLEAR family,
the LACTOSE in mother's milk. "

Find the / r / pillow and move its sound through your body.

"The HEROIC Pinot NOIR is MORE VIRILE NEARLY FURRY
going to down."

Find the / ə / pillow and combine it with the / r / pillow forming a little sound that begins with / ə / and ends with / r / . This will be something like the "er" sound in MOTHER. Let this little sound move through your body. Throw /ə/ and / r / back on the pile and find / ɚ / , the sound in MOTHER and UNDERSTAND. Notice the tiny /ˑ/ perched up on the /ə/. Remember, this is a little sound. Find it in your body.

"The TENOR sings tonight and the dancing OTTER is going on
with the ACTOR from down UNDER."

Now combine / ɚ / with some other sounds and let their vibrations come to
life in your body. Then say a line using each sound from *The Undiapered Filefish*.
Get the / ɪ / pillow. Let the sound begin with / ɪ / and end with / ɚ / . Get physical with it. You will arrive at a sound that is something like EAR.

Try this line:

"I want to CLEAR the air, buy you a BEER. I think you're first
TIER. I'm interested in your CAREER."

Follow the same steps with / ɛ / and / ɚ / .

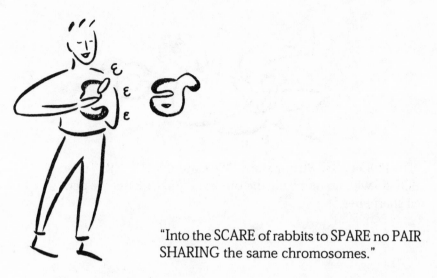

"Into the SCARE of rabbits to SPARE no PAIR SHARING the same chromosomes."

"He SCARRED records, was afraid to ride in a CAR, did HARM to our number one SHARK."

"It's from that SWARM of WARTHOGS that TORE through town last week when the FORMAL dance was SORT of winding down."

"The POOR ASSURE our plans. We cannot be DOUR. Those BOORS with no home but the office, no ALLURE but the pencil sharpener."

"Don't REQUIRE me to INQUIRE about whom you ADMIRE."

"The FOYER is prepared. SAWYER will meet the LAWYER at the door."

"I was just about to SCOUR the SHOWER curtain when you came in. What lovely FLOWERS."

Find the /ɝ/ pillow. This is the "er" sound in JERK, the "ir" sound in GIRL. Say this line from the play:

"When that JERK LURKS in SEARCH of this collection of mollusks, I shall STIR his cornflakes."

Now having felt the /ɝ/ sound in words, send /ɝ/ vibrations through your body.

When you're finished, throw / ɝ / back on the pile. Now once again, stir up your language soup. Not just with your hands and arms, but your whole body. Let any and all parts of your body randomly encounter sounds. Let the sounds move freely through your body. Savor them, indulge them, enjoy them, use your whole range of expression from high to low, from long to short. What a picnic!

Now pick up a pillow and toss it to someone. As it releases from your hands, let its sound release from your body. Imagine the pillow is propelled through space on the fuel of your vibrations. For the pillows with long-lasting sounds, your voice can careen all the way across the space with them; the pillows with shorter lasting sounds will need you to release their vibrations several times in order to sustain their trip through space. As you catch a pillow that someone else has thrown to you, let your body catch its vibrations so that whether you catch or throw a pillow, its vibrations release through your voice. Continue randomly flinging and catching these pillows and their sounds until you feel an easy recognition of all the phonetic symbols.

Sounds come in many shapes and sizes. They can be grouped together by personality types; the length of their duration, the articulators used to form them, and the way the breath flows through them.

Separate your consonant pillows into the two groups illustrated below. Play with each pillow in one group, then in the other. What does each group of sounds have in common? How are they different from the sounds in the other group?

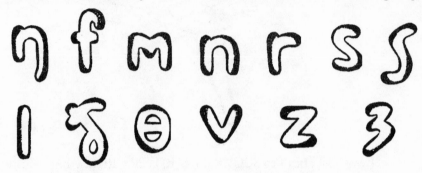

The sounds in this group are called "continuants." Their sounds can go on, and on, and on, or they can be as short as you want them to be. When you play with these sounds, let them have this autonomy; depending on what they want to express they can be long, short, or anywhere in between.

These sounds are called "stop plosives." They have a very short duration. In order to form them, the flow of breath is STOPPED between two articulating surfaces for a split second. As the breath flow resumes, it "explodes" the two surfaces apart.

/b / and /p /are formed between the lips. They are sometimes called "bilabial plosives."

/ d / and /t / are formed between the tip of the tongue and the gum ridge. They are sometimes called "alveolar plosives."

/g / and /k / are formed between the soft palate and back of tongue. They are sometimes called "lingua-velar plosives."

If you try to make these sounds last longer, they lose their essential quality. Whenever you play with these sounds keep them short; let them be what they inherently are, so that they can make their own unique contribution to language.

Explore the sounds in the following group. What do they have in common?

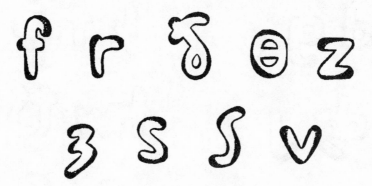

The sounds in this group are formed with a narrow stream of breath or voice between two articulating surfaces. Because of the resultant "friction," they are sometimes called "fricatives."

/ð/ , /θ/	are caused by friction between the tip of the tongue and the top front teeth.
/s/ , /z/, /ʃ/ , /ʒ/	are caused by friction between the tongue and the gum ridge.
/f/ , /v/	are caused by friction between the top front teeth and the lower lip.
/r/	is caused by friction between the tip of the tongue and the hard palate.

Play with these two pillows:

Can you feel the explosion *and* friction in these sounds? Each of these sounds is actually two sounds combined. The first component is a "plosive," and the second component is a "fricative." The resultant sound is sometimes called an "affricate."

Explore the sounds in the two groups below. What does each group of sounds have in common?

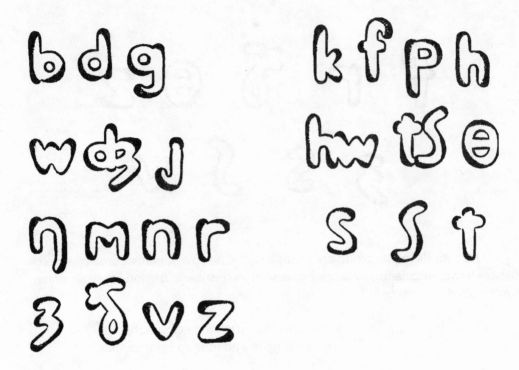

In the group on the left, all the sounds are VOICED. In the group on the right, they're all VOICELESS.

Arrange the pillows in the following pairs. Work with one pair at a time. How are these pairs alike? How are they different?

In these pairs, both sounds are formed in the same way. One is voiced and the other is voiceless. Such voiced and voiceless counterparts are sometimes called "consonant cognates."

Play with these three pillows for awhile. What characteristic do their sounds share?

In each of these sounds, the mouth passage is closed:

/m /   at the lips.

/n /   at the tongue and the gum ridge.

/ŋ /   at the soft palate and back of tongue.

These sounds are called "nasal continuants." The breath stream is sent through the nose and the sound duration can continue indefinitely. Although these sounds are called "nasal" and the air flow is indeed through the nose, don't let the sound gather exclusively in the nose. Feel the vibrations gathering primarily between the surfaces that close off the mouth passage.

How is this sound different from the others?

The sound /l / is released through the sides of the mouth, over the tongue. It is sometimes called a "lateral" sound.

Where in your mouth are these sounds formed?

These three sounds formed between the soft palate and back of tongue are sometimes called "velar" or "lingua-velar." Let your entire body be moved by these sounds as if you were one big soft palate and back of tongue. As the body moves, feel it first gathering the vibrations and energy of the sound, and then sending them out into the air.

What surfaces come together to make these two sounds?

These two sounds, made between the top front teeth and lower lip are sometimes called "labial-dental." Let your body take on the personality of your bottom lip and top-teeth as the sound moves through you.

How do you form these sounds?

These sounds are made using the top and bottom lip and are sometimes called "bi-labials." Imagine your whole body as two enormous lips and let these sounds express through you.

Unlike most consonants, the three sounds above can each stand alone as a syllable—as in the words SPASM, LITTLE, and SEVEN. When acting as a syllable, they are transcribed with a dot underneath / m̩ /, / l̩ /, / n̩ /.

Where in your mouth are these sounds formed?

The tip of the tongue is at the gum ridge behind the top front teeth to form these sounds. They are sometimes called "alveolar" sounds. One by one, using the pillows, apply these sounds to your body. Let your body take on the sensations you feel in your mouth between these two surfaces. Let each sound move freely through your body.

Which articulators form these sounds?

These sounds are formed between your top front teeth and the tip of the tongue. They are sometimes called "lingua dental" sounds. Let the sound releasing through these surfaces sweep through your body.

Briefly, here are definitions of the terms used above:

Fricatives: sounds made with "friction" between two surfaces, such as

/f/, /v/, /s/, /z/, /ʃ/, /ʒ/, /θ/, /ð/, /r/.

Plosives: sounds made with an "explosion" between two surfaces such as /b/, /p/, /d/, /t/, /g/, /k/.

Affricatives: sounds made of a fricative and a plosive combined /dʒ/, /tʃ/.

Alveolar: sounds formed with the tip of the tongue and the gum ridge. /d/, /t/, /l/, /n/, /s/, /z/, /ʃ/, /ʒ/.

Labial: sounds formed with the lips. /m/, /p/, /b/.

Lingua-velar: sounds formed between the soft palate and back of tongue. /g/, /k/, /ŋ/.

Labial-dental: sounds formed between the top front teeth and bottom lip. /f/, /v/.

I have a friend who says that "teaching is for teachers." If that's the case, then these terms are much more for speech teachers than they are for the actors they teach. It's much more important for actors to know on an experiential level what's going on in their mouths as they speak, than it is for them to know the clinical terms for each type of sound. Latin terms like "bi-labial" create an academic distance between the expert and the artist—why not say "two-lipped?"

When a simple little "r" is called a "post alveolar-fricative continuant*," things are getting pretty complicated! (*Speak With Distinction, Applause Books, 1992)

Play with these two groups of pillows. How are the vowels in each group different?

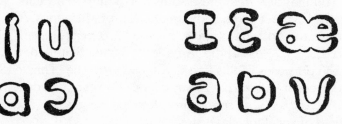

The vowels on the left are called "long vowels." As you play with them, you can extend their sound through a long sigh, or let them happen a little quicker;

however, if you make them too short, they lose their essence and begin to sound like short vowels. Don't let them get too short.

The vowels on the right are called "short vowels." These sounds cannot sustain themselves for any length of time without losing their essence and becoming some other sound. As you play with them, you need to re-release them many times if you want them to travel through your whole body. They simply can't sweep through you on one long extended sound. Keep them short.

Group your pillows into the following pairs:

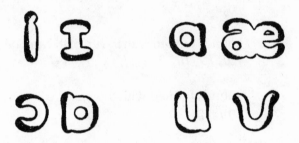

Play with each pair separately, letting the two sounds express themselves through your body. What difference do you find between the sounds in each pair?

Although the two sounds from each pair aren't formed identically, they are from the same family. They're similar, but each has its own personality. The ones on the left are long, outgoing vowels: /i /, /ɑ /, /u /, /ɔ /, and the ones on the right are short, quick vowels: /ɪ /, /æ /, /ʊ /, /ɒ /. Let them have their unique personality traits as you play with them.

A Note on /a/ and /ɒ/

Two sounds that are not universally used in a U.S. accent are /ɒ / as in ODD, known as the "Short O," and /a / as in DANCE, which is called the "Middle A."

Whatever familiarity you have with these sounds may have to do with what part of the U.S. you come from. Some northeastern U.S. speakers use both of these sounds. You may also hear these sounds in Southern accents. Although a lot of people in the US don't particularly use these pronunciations, /ɒ / and /a / are distinguishing features of what is know as "Good American Speech," also called "Good Speech for Classic Texts" or the "American Theater Standard."

For the purposes of this book, you can view the "Theater Standard" as just another US accent and learn it *as* an accent. You can include it in your repertoire without adopting it as your sole approach to speaking classic texts. There are *many* worthy ways of speaking classic texts.

Here is a comparison of the use of /ɒ / and /a / in the American Theater Standard accent, versus /ɑ / and /æ / in a more colloquial U.S. accent:

The word ASK in the "Theater Standard" is spoken with the Middle A /a / and is transcribed as /ask /.

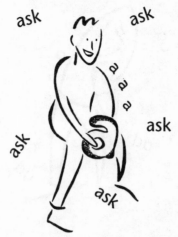

However, a very common U.S. pronunciation of ASK is with the Short A /æsk /

In the "Theater Standard" accent, the word ODD is pronounced with the Short O /ɒ /.

Yet, a very common U.S. pronunciation is to use the Broad A /ɑ / rather than the Short O /ɒ /.

The symbol /ɒ / is the same as /ɑ / only turned upside down and backwards. Watch out that you don't mistakenly use one in place of the other when transcribing. For those of you who don't use /ɒ / and /ɑ / in your own accents, I can't really teach them to you on paper, but I'll try to steer you in their direction.

First, let us deal with / ɒ /, as in this line from the play:

"WHAT COMEDY this NOD to the POSSIBLE INVOLVEMENT
OF GOD is the religion OF the ODD COLLEGE SCHOLAR."

/ɒ / is similar to /ɔ / but shorter in duration and different in the positioning of the tongue. You can think of /ɒ / as halfway between /ɔ / and /ɑ / .

Say / ɔ / and notice the position of the tongue and lips.

Now say /ɑ / and again notice where the tongue and lips are.

Now find a position of the tongue and lips that is halfway between /ɔ / and /ɑ / . Let the sound be very short.

You'll probably arrive at something like /ɒ /.

Play with the /ɑ / and /ɒ / pillows. Let your body compare them. Say these two lines using /ɑ / in both of them:

"I did SPA work in the PLAZA and found myself among the SUAVEST FATHERS in town."

"WHAT COMEDY to the POSSIBLE INVOLVEMENT OF GOD is the religion OF the ODD COLLEGE SCHOLAR."

Now that you've said both lines using the vowel /ɑ /, switch to the Theater Standard accent by using /ɒ / instead of /ɑ / in the second line, "WHAT COMEDY..." Two sounds that can help you find /a /, the Middle A are /æ / and /ɑ /.

Say /æ / and notice where your tongue is.

Now say /ɑ / and notice that your tongue has lowered.

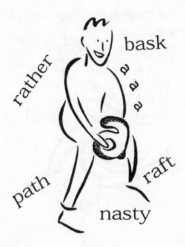

To make /a / the Middle A sound, find a position of your tongue that is half-way between /æ / and /ɑ /. Let the sound be short, like /æ /. You'll end up with something like /a /.

Say these lines from the play using /æ / in both of them:

> "I RANG the LAD AND he used LANGUAGE AS though it were
> AN AX."

> "I'd RATHER BASK in the PATH of my PASTOR than fight a
> RAFT of NASTY bowls of chowder.

Now switch to the "Theater Standard" accent in the second line, "I'd RATHER BASK..." by changing from /æ / to /a /.

I've certainly seen plenty of good classical work where the actors made no effort to "standardize" the way they pronounced words in order to suit the text. Whether you find any use for /ɒ / and /a / in your work is up to your own artistry and the demands of the production. However, it's necessary to know both these sounds when working with accents.

In a British accent for instance, Middle A words like RATHER, BASK, PATH, PASTOR, RAFT and NASTY are pronounced with the vowel /ɑ /: /rɑðə /, /bɑsk/ /pɑθ /, /pɑstə /, /rɑft /, /nɑstɪ /.

Other short-voweled "a" words, such as RANG, LAD, LANGUAGE, AX however, don't change in this way. This could cause confusion and an inaccurate accent if you didn't know Middle A words from Short A words.

Similarly, in a British accent the vowel /ɒ / is used where a lot of U.S. speakers would use the vowel /ɑ /. For instance, the vowel in ODD changes from the Broad A /ɑ / in a U.S. accent to the Short O /ɒ / in a British accent. If you didn't know the difference between /ɑ / and /ɒ / the same confusion could result.

It helps to know some rules of spelling in order to distinguish the Short O /ɒ / and the Middle A /a / from other sounds.

Rules are made to be broken, but spelling can be a big clue. /ɒ / words are almost always spelled with O: COMEDY, GOD, SCHOLAR.

This includes some words spelled with O that most US speakers pronounce /ʌ/ such as: OF, FROM, WHAT, WAS.

Short O words can also be spelled with WA: WASH, WATCH, WHAT, WAS.

Below are the general rules for identifying /ɒ/ and /ɑ/ words (for more detailed information, consult a pronunciation dictionary.)

In brief:

Short O words are:

> transcribed with the symbol /ɒ/ in "Theater Standard" or /ɑ/ in General American
>
> usually spelled with O as in COMEDY, GOD, SCHOLAR
>
> sometimes spelled with WA
>
> often pronounced as /ɑ/ in the US
>
> in the case of certain words, pronounced as /ʌ/ in the U.S. —OF, FROM, WAS

Here is a brief list of Short O words: COMEDY, GOD, SCHOLAR, ODD, STOP, BOB, FOG, LOCK, POP, LOT, WASH, WATCH, WHAT, WAS, OF, and FROM.

Middle A words are:

> transcribed with the symbol /a/ in "Theater Standard" or /æ/ in General American

always spelled with "a"—PATH, PAST, RATHER, CAN'T, LAUGH, STAFF,
PASS, SAMPLE, DEMAND (If an "a" word has one of the consonant
endings of the above words, it could be a "Middle A" word)
words spelled with "a" followed by these consonants—with many exceptions (when in doubt, refer to a pronunciation dictionary)—f, s, st,
sk, th, nt, nd, mpl, ns

Here are a few words with consonant endings from the above list which are considered Middle A words: AUNT, GRASS, FRANCE, PLANT, COMMAND, DE-MAND, EXAMPLE, SAMPLE, LATHER and CAN'T.

There are hundreds of other Middle A words that you can recognize by their consonant endings. Be aware that there are many exceptions to the Middle A rule. Here are a few words with the consonant endings from the above list that are considered Short A words: ANT, CRASS, ROMANCE, PANTS, HAND, LAMP and GATHER.

Part Two

Games

Once you are familiar with the symbols, you can use the pillows to play games. At the University of Missouri-Kansas City, my students and I invented some games that I will pass on to you. Feel free to adapt these games to the needs of your group. Once you start to play them, variations and entirely new games will emerge. These games will help you to:

> Retain the symbol for each sound and speed up recognition time
> Open your imagination, emotions, and intellect to a deeper relationship
>   with each sound
> Tune your body to the inherent energy of each sound
> Break down language and trace it to its roots
> Find the origin of the impulse to speak within yourself
> Listen with your entire body

Have fun!

Game One: Inventing Language

Begin with a pile of pillows on the floor. Each player takes a pillow and moves its sound through their body. Once the sound is well established the player, lets it move their body around the room Moving through the space, the player will encounter other players with other pillows and sounds.

Still letting sound move the body, the player joins one or more other players to form a cluster of sounds. Within the cluster, one by one, each player releases their sound, at first randomly, but play continues until an order of sounds emerges. Once the order is apparent, all players begin to release the entire sequence of sounds in unison. This sequence may be a jumble of language or it may contain an actual word (or words).

Repeat the sequence as many times as it can sustain the interest of the group. As the sequence is repeated, it may start to take on a meaning or emotional life that the group can play with. Continue to let the sound move the body, allowing the pillows to make contact not only with the body of the player holding it but other players' bodies as well.

When this sequence has run its course, the players discard their pillows and let themselves be drawn to another one. Let this new sound lead to a new cluster and a new sequence.

Game Two: The Diphthong Game

Players form a circle. This game uses a pile of vowel pillows only. Someone is chosen captain. The captain picks up a pillow and gets its sound moving his/her body. This pillow is then passed around the circle, each player releasing its sound through their body. Once the pillow has circulated through the entire group, it is placed on the floor in the center of the circle. The captain then grabs a second pillow. This new sound is combined with the sound in the center of the circle to form a diphthong. As the pillow is passed around the circle, each player combines it with the first sound, releasing the resultant diphthong through the body. Once the diphthong is strongly established, everyone can release the sound in unison regardless of who has the pillow at that moment.

When the captain feels that the diphthong has been thoroughly explored, he/she will discard the circulating pillow and replace it with another pillow that, in combination with the center pillow will create a new diphthong. Continue until all the vowels have been used in combination with the center pillow at which time the captain will replace it with a new center pillow, and the game continues. When using diphthong pillows in combination with other vowel pillows, a triphthong (three vowels combined) / aɪo / for instance, or a quadrathong (four vowels combined) / aɪoə /, for instance, will result.

Variations: "The Blend Game": The same steps as above, but with consonants only rather than vowels only. "Random Combining": The same game as above, using all the pillows.

Game Three: Passing Sound Around

Everyone stands in a circle with all the pillows in the center. Someone is chosen to be captain. Each player picks up a pillow and runs it all over the body, releasing its sound. When enough time has passed for each player to be completely absorbed in his/her pillow, the captain initiates a rotation in which each player passes the pillow and sound to the player on their left. By running the pillow over the neighbor's body (almost like painting the sound onto the neighbor—the sound being the paint, the letter, the brush) everyone gradually traverses out of the old sound into the new sound and eventually takes hold of the new pillow, releasing the old pillow into the hands of the neighbor. Each player explores the new sound until the captain again initiates the rotation. The rotation continues in this way until all the pillows have circulated to each player. The captain then initiates discarding these pillows (outside of the circle) and getting new pillows from the central pile for a second series of rotation.

Game Four: Drawn to Sound

The pillows are spread out all over the floor. The players spread themselves out around the room. The game begins with each player spotting a different pillow across the room. Each player lets the sound of the selected pillow release through the voice and move the body, letting the body be drawn toward the pillow. The player then meets the pillow, picks it up, and moves its sound around the body for as long as the player likes. The player may meet other players and get into body/sound conversations with them. When ready, the player drops the pillow to the floor and spots another pillow across the room. Again, the player is drawn to the pillow, and the game continues.

Game Five: The Soundalogue

One person plays at a time. The rest of the group assists that player. The pillows are in a tight pile on the floor. The player stands in front of the pile and speaks a well-memorized monologue. All others position themselves around the pile facing the player. When the player gets to the end of the monologue, he/she loops back to the beginning and goes through it again. When the group is confident that the player is completely involved in the monologue, they begin to grab letters from the pile and hand them, one by one, to the player in any random order. The player continues, going for the sense of the speech, but instead of using the actual words of the monologue, the player uses the random sounds handed to him/her. The group must constantly hand new letters to the player. This process must go at the speed of the thought of the monologue. The pace is fast. No time for deliberation. The sounds of the letters *become* the text of the monologue for the player. The player must keep the whole body alive and responsive to each sound. When the player reaches the end of the speech in this way, he/she immediately returns to the beginning and speaks the actual words again.

Because the player has fed every sound of the language through the body in random combinations while doing the speech, old patterned ways of saying the speech can be broken, making way for new possibilities when the speech is finally said in the actual words again.

Game Six: Improv Game A

Two or more players outline a brief scenario, circumstance, and action for an improvised scene. Choose a scene with lots of verbal interaction. The pillows are placed on a large table in front of the players. Rather than using literal language, the scene is played out with random sounds picked up from the pillows on the table. The players have the freedom to voice and discard the pillows in fast succession or linger with one sound as suits the purpose of communicating thoughts and feelings. As in the other games, players must allow sound to move their bodies, not only their own sounds, but also their partners' sounds. The players must listen and speak with their whole bodies. They should let themselves be changed by their partner's sound and change their partner with their sound. There will be times in the scene when players rub a pillow's sound over their own body and their partner's as well.

As the players discard the pillows by letting them drop to the floor, the rest of the group is responsible for returning them to the table and keeping them well mixed so that the players get a chance to use as many sounds as possible.

Game Seven: Improv Game B

A variation on the "Improv Game" is to place the pillows in a pile on the floor rather than on a table. The players lie on the floor, immersing themselves in the pile of pillows. There is much more freedom for random contact with the pillows using any part of the body. This is a way to get beyond finding the pillows and moving them around the body with just the hands. The improv can take on a greater physicality. There are endless possibilities for body to body and pillow to body contact. This improv will be less literal than Improv A. Physical actions are abstracted; the body *becomes* sound.

Game Eight: Symphony

The more players the better for this game. One player will be the conductor and the rest will be members of the orchestra. Orchestra members have pillows as their instruments, which they play with their entire bodies. The conductor can arrange the orchestra in any way desired. For instance, short vowels, long vowels, and diphthongs in separate sections, or front vowels and back vowels in their own sections. Continuant consonants and stop consonants in different sections or voiced, and voiceless consonants in their own sections, etc. The conductor can choose to recreate an actual piece of music, or perhaps choose a general theme: "The Symphony of Love," "The Symphony of Destruction." The conductor guides the orchestra, sections, and soloists through the piece. Using gesture and even sound, the conductor can indicate loud, soft, crescendo, decrescendo, legato, and staccato.

In a variation on this game, the conductor chooses a monologue and has a forty-three member orchestra so that all the pillows are used, making all the sounds in the language available. The conductor leads the orchestra through the monologue sound by sound.

Game Nine: Finding Your Monologue

One player at a time. Spread the pillows all over the floor in plain view of the player. The player will work with a well-memorized monologue.

The player goes through a speech one sound at a time, releasing each sound repeatedly until finding the pillow for that sound. The player moves to it and makes body contact with it, and then moves on to the second sound in the speech, searching for the pillow for that sound, contacting it and so on. The object is to go as fast as possible and make as much sense of the speech as possible. The player can either stand or move along the floor crawling or slithering.

A variation of this game is to search for each pillow, but only release its sound once body contact has been made with it. Again, aim at going as quickly as possible and playing the speech as fully as possible.

Game Ten: Go Fish

Players are separated into teams. Each team is given one word. The word chosen for each team should not have any sounds in it that are also used in the other team's words. For instance:

Team 1:	search
Team 2:	find
Team 3:	look

Each member of the team is assigned one sound and must find the pillow for that sound. The pillows are spread out over the entire floor space. The players enter the dimly lit space with their eyes either closed or in a very soft focus. It is cheating to find the pillow by sight. It must be found by touch. The players move along the floor and release the sounds of any pillows they encounter. If it is not the pillow each is looking for, it is discarded and the search continues. When they find their sounds, they keep the pillow and continue releasing its sound and letting it move their bodies until they meet up with the other members of their team (whose sounds they will hear and move toward) and the sounds of the word are reunited.

In a variation of this game, single players can be responsible for all the sounds of an entire word, eventually meeting up with the other players to form sentences. Again, it is important that the chosen words don't have sounds that repeat in other players' words. Otherwise, every player won't be able to find all of the sounds.

Part Three

Good Speech

It is a natural thing that man should speak;
But whether this or that way, Nature leaves
To your election, as it pleases you.
For mortal usages are like leaves on trees;
They fall and others grow.—Dante's Paradiso

You have played with all the pillows in this pile. You've joined their sounds together in countless combinations, allowed them to express through you in new and unexpected ways, and examined their essential qualities—their differences and similarities. Now you can start putting sounds back into language, exploring the sounds of your own accent and the accents of other people. The work on accents will be centered around the way that you, yourself speak. No "key word list" of "correct" pronunciations will be imposed on you. No "standard" of speech will be offered for you to measure yourself against.

The original purpose of the International Phonetic Alphabet was to fix language, not to explore it; to assign pronunciations that were considered preferable or even universal. Yet, no word exists with just one pronunciation accepted by all. Any standard of pronunciation is biased. Favoring one way of speaking can discount another.

Setting standards can force so-called regional accents and dialects into the fringes of credibility. If my accent does not reflect the accepted voice of intelligence, reason, and authority, I can live with the stigma, change the way that I speak, or go to greater lengths to be heard. An unheard voice may seek other venues of expression—perhaps creative, perhaps destructive.

U.S. theater encompasses many regions and cultures. There can be no single arbiter of "good speech." No single accent is most suitable for speaking Shakespeare.

Even so, an authoritarian approach to pronunciation exists in the arenas of education, mass media, and especially the theater.

To this day many actors speak in the style of nineteenth century elocutionists and phoneticians when acting in plays by Shakespeare and other "classical" playwrights.

This way of speaking, widely taught in actor training programs is variously known as "Good American Speech," "American Theater Standard," "Mid-Atlantic Speech" and "Good Speech for Classic Texts."

"Classic texts" in this context refers to: verse plays (like Shakespeare), translated plays, non-contemporary plays that don't require accents, and plays set in imagined or historically distanced places (like the bland non-accent heard in Biblical epic films.)

You have already explored two sounds that are distinctive features of "Good Speech for Classic Texts" in chapter one: / a / in words like ASK, and / ɒ / in words like ODD. Some of the other sounds used in this speech pattern are: / ju / in words like DUE, NEWS, SUIT, TUNE, and LUNAR, and the removal or "R coloring" between a vowel and a consonant as in the word HEART, / hɑːt /, and at the end of a word as in the word CAR, / kɑː /. These four sounds together create an accent that is quite different from the accents of most Americans. While the sounds of American English evolve over generations, the sounds of American Classical Theater remain largely in a time-warp.

Before accepting this speech pattern as the "good" way to speak classic texts, you may want to know a little more about it: its origin, and societal implications.

At the heart of this seemingly innocuous speech pattern are the values of Victorian imperialism. "Good Speech for Classic Texts" is modeled on the speech of upper-class white British men of eighty years ago. Although blindly (deafly) accepted as mere theatrical convention, it is inherently racist, sexist, and elitist, not to mention, antiquated.

To trace the development of "American Theater Standard" we need to go back to the early part of this century, when "elocution" was going strong. In England, in 1916, speech teacher and phonetician Daniel Jones was analyzing and documenting the pronunciation and speaking style of southern British men who had attended public boarding school. This accent, acquired, or "received" through education, is called "received pronunciation," RP for short. Americans easily recognized this accent as "Upper Class British." The preface to Jones's *English Pronunciation Dictionary* states that "Those whose dialect differs considerably from RP will make concessions to it..." and that "...every dialect has its interest and appeal, but one who knows only his dialect finds himself at a disadvantage in social life...." and may have an impaired sense of the aesthetic of English literature. That RP or any class-defined standard is the inherent aesthetic measure of English literature is an outrageous assumption. Yet, in the American theater of today, this assumption prevails in the form of "Good Speech for Classic Texts."

At around the time that Jones was compiling his pronouncing dictionary of RP, a similar way of speaking was being promulgated in the U.S. by William Tilly, Jones's teacher who had recently come to America. Tilly's so-called "good American speech" would become known in actor training parlance as "Good Speech for Classic Texts," or the "American Theater Standard."

The article below, by Dudley Knight, head of actor-training at the University of California, Irvine, was originally published in the Voice and Speech Teacher's Association newsletter. It traces the history of "good American speech" from William Tilly, to a generation of American teachers.

William Tilly and "Good Speech"

Speech training for actors in the United States has been defined and dominated, for the past fifty years, by Edith Warman Skinner.

For several decades at Carnegie-Mellon, and then late in her career at the Juilliard School, Edith Skinner's passion for what she termed "Good American Speech," and her demanding pedagogical style—multiplied by the large number of theater speech instructors she trained—formed to a large extent the verbal patterns of several generations of American classical actors. For many years most of these actors, accepted without question the tenets of the speech pattern that Skinner prescribed. But of late, these criteria for "Standard Speech" have been questioned, debated, championed, rejected, by a growing number of theater trainers.

The prevailing assumption in this debate has been that the pattern in question was of Skinner's own formulation. Although Skinner herself never made such a claim. In fact what Skinner carried so effectively into American theater training was a speech pattern specifically formulated by her teacher, William Tilly, with whom she studied in the late twenties and early thirties. That this should be so is no small paradox, since Tilly had no interest in the theater whatever.

William Tilly was a phonetician, one of the early members of the International Phonetic Association. Born in Australia in 1860, Tilly studied with Wilhelm Vietor, the famed German philologist, who brought him into the Association Phonetique, along with the English phonetic pioneer Henry Sweet.

He spent most of his career in Germany, where he founded a successful school to teach German language and culture to English students. His school was closed at the start of the First World War, and for a time Tilly was interned by the German government. Upon his release he traveled to England, and then to America, where he became an instructor in phonetics in the Columbia University extension program in 1918.

Tilly was very much a man of the nineteenth century. His view of teaching, his sense of phonetics as a new science, his social perspective, and cultural ideals, were all shaped within a world in which the British Empire was at its zenith. His pedagogy was shaped further by its immersion within a German tradition of scholarship: one of his students in Germany was Daniel Jones, the dominant figure in British phonetics during the first half of this century. Jones commented that most of Tilly's students were young men who had been through the English university system, but still had no idea how to study. "Tilly taught them how to work" noted Jones, with appropriate emphasis. Students of Edith Skinner doubtless remember a similar sense of rigor.

At the age of fifty-eight, Tilly began his teaching career in the United States, a career that lasted seventeen years until his death in 1935. He had developed a distinctive approach to phonetics, one that was not shared by many in his field (including Jones), a distinctive ideology of speech standards, and a distinctive pedagogy. All of these were adopted by his devoted coterie some might say—in fact did say—"cult" of students, which included Edith Skinner, Margeret Pendergast McLean, and Alice Hermes. Tilly himself published only one article, in which these three areas are only touched upon, but his students published frequently, and at least five of them produced textbooks, all of which expound Tilly's ideas in detail and in more or less identical fashion.

Tilly believed strongly in narrow phonetic transcription, a focus which placed him at variance from most of his colleagues in American speech teaching at the time. They were more interested in the broad transcription of speech sounds at the phonetic level. Tilly held that only narrow transcription could notate sound changes and variations in enough detail to be of practical use in linguistic research. He pioneered the use of nonsense word dictation, and of dictation in languages other than English. The evidence in Skinner's own notebooks when she studied with Tilly show that much time was spent in philological inquiry, and in explorations of phonetic transcriptions in different languages, many of them archaic. However, it must be noted also that the transcriptions of detailed speech sound patterns in Skinner's notebooks do not seem to be based on descriptive reproduction of sounds by native speakers. Instead they seem to be based on arbitrary rules of utterance in the language under investigation. So Tilly's interest in detail of sound production seems to be contravened by his equally strong desire for uniformity and correctness. Every language it would appear, has its "standard."

Tilly's pedagogy follows from this same set of concerns. It was, from all evidence, autocratic and highly demanding. Students were seated in his classroom according to their ranking in transcription ability. Margaret McLean, Tilly's assistant, held the coveted first chair, first row, for years. Edith Skinner used to tell her students that it took her over five years of study to get to the second chair. Students often brought the requisite six sharpened No. 2 pencils to Tilly's classes regularly for up to a decade. Neatness of transcription and correct formation of phonetic symbols were given a high priority. Tilly's ideology of speech standards remains his most enduring and his most controversial legacy. He and his followers believed passionately in a "world standard" of English speech. This specifically—a class-based speech pattern, for the use of Americans aspiring to upward social mobility. A crucial part of the ideology of "world standard" English was that it represented no indigenous speech pattern in the English-speaking world. It was, instead, a pattern supposedly spoken by persons, of whatever nationality, who were variously described as being "cultured," "cultivated," or "educated." (That these terms were used by Tilly's disciples in a way that would make a social scientist even in the 1920s blush, was of no apparent concern to them.) But to American linguists outside of Tilly's circle, the pattern was immediately identifiable as southern British. This observation was corroborated by the fact that there was no such ideology of a "world standard" of speech in England, even in the decade where standards of RP were being formulated and hotly debated. After all, 1920s Oxbridge speakers didn't need to concern themselves with what their colonies, past and present, might be aspiring to speak; they were already speaking it.

During Tilly's lifetime his idiosyncratic system of phonetic transcription and his espousal of a "world standard" of English caused him to be isolated from both linguists and speech instructors. Even though today's linguistic phoneticians have embraced a narrow transcription system, for most uses. The one place where his theories have endured virtually unchanged in the almost sixty years since he died is in the training of American classical actors. Through the influence of his students Margeret Pendergast McLean, Alice Hermes, and most especially, Edith Skinner.

For a complete understanding of the speech pattern referred to in this article, see *Speak With Distinction* by Edith Skinner, Applause 1992.

When I hear "Good American Speech" I have a sense of neutral non-offensiveness. The speaker is rooted in the blandness of being from no particular place, with no particular background.

In the multi-cultural theater of today, the use of pronunciation standards is being rethought on both sides of the Atlantic. Intelligibility and vocal freedom are far more important than uniform pronunciation. In cases where similar pronunciation among characters is germane to the story of the play, it needn't be assumed that "Good American Speech" is the best model for unifying the speech of the actors. In plays with a hierarchy of royalty and nobility, using "Good Speech for Classic Texts" creates a myth that "courtly speech" is affected and fastidious. A king doesn't *need* to sound kingly. On the other end of the social scale, lower-class characters are often made to sound quaint and rustic. In the bargain the colloquial speech patterns of the audience are banished from the stage. "Good speech" as a measure of status carries a very loaded subliminal message to the audience. "Good American Speech" has been called a "compromise accent"—a sort of goodwill effort to meet British stage speech at least halfway. The underlying sentiment of this compromise is that indiginous American speech isn't good enough for the classics.

> The way people cast a play! As if all cooks were fat, all farm-ers tough, all statesmen stately! As if all lovers were pretty! As if all great orators had beautiful voices! "That actor looks like a king." What does that mean? Must all kings look like Edward VII? "This one has a commanding presence." How many ways of commanding are there? "That woman is too noble-looking to play Mother Courage." Too noble? Go look at the fishwives.—Bertolt Brecht

According to a recent Census report, one out of seven U.S. residents (over thirty-one million people) speaks a language other than English in the home. The majority of these people are also fluent in English. With the influence of speech patterns from 329 different languages, we're in for great shifts in the sound of American English. If English indeed survives as the primary language of our culture, the current standards of "good speech" must give way to, and make room for, the New American Accent—whatever that might be. We may be on the brink of a re-naissance of the language to match that of the Elizabethan age: In which the collec-tive tongue of English will stretch, loosen and reshape itself, asserting the expressivity of its many and varied speakers. What an exciting time this could be for the theater!

Setting standards has created a climate of intolerance for the innovative voices of our culture: The accents of immigrants, and the so-called sub-standard dialects of people from urban and rural communities, can be difficult to hear over the op-pressive din of "correctness." When an audience must train its ears to listen for the truth behind an actor's artificial stage diction, the theater is becoming too highbrow: The rich diverseness of society's voices is not represented. "Good Speech for Clas-sic Texts" as a vernacular is extinct; it is a speech pattern of "dead white men." Its prevalence in the classical theater precludes the possibility of a culturally diverse au-dience. When (as in Shakespeare's time) classic texts are spoken colloquially, in the actors' native accents, a window of personal identification opens to the audience. The words don't sound antiquated; they sound alive again.

Does "Good Speech for Classic Texts" serve the language and characters of contemporary American dramatists? Not that I can see. Is it then a way of speaking relegated to the classics because the way most Americans speak doesn't ring true as "heightened," "elevated," "heroic?" Only if we want to distance ourselves from the classics, straining to hear muffled voices from another age that speak and feel things we would never dream of speaking and feeling ourselves.

The emotional and intellectual demands of classic texts go far beyond the casual (if not lazy) investment level of everyday speaking. Standard speech is insufficient to restore fullness and vitality to these texts; there is more to heightened language than heightened speech patterns. If a student actor's regional accent is out of balance with the world of the play and the speech of the other actors, he must be given some latitude (along with a daily regimen of voice-freeing exercises) even if it seems to be at the expense of the production. If pronunciations differing from the standard are constantly "corrected", his efforts to shift them will almost certainly lead to vocal tension and at the same time pull him out of the reality of the play. Grappling with large emotions and universal truth will exercise and challenge the voice, stretching the actor away from the limitations of regional influence. It is not an actor's slightly different formation of vowels or use of consonants that renders his performance inaccessible to a wide audience. A limiting regional accent is merely the by-product of patterns of tension frozen into the vocal tract. As the speech structures are rehabilitated through tension-releasing exercises, the limitations of nasality, stridency, gutteralness, monotone, drawl, under-articulation, and hard r's will fall away leaving subtler traces of the formerly "heavy" or "thick" accent. At this point in the actor's (person's) development, the deep muscle release having been accomplished, a little ear-training can help fine tune pronunciations into harmony with the world of a given play and the speech of the other actors.

If speech is dealt with too early in the actor's development, it becomes a veneer over muscular blockage. While speech work (done before the voice is free) may result in a more "open sound," it only replaces a convex muscular obstruction with a rigidly concave openness. An open sound is achieved, but only through shifting a constricted vocal apparatus to one held rigidly open. It is this very rigidity that will rob the actor of the subtle nuance of thought and feeling. In a state of tension, it is difficult to recognize a useful acting impulse much less know how to follow one. A good actor is multiphonological, not limited to any single way of speaking—able to achieve a maximum effect with a minimum of effort.

What one group calls "good speech" may seem ridiculous or excluding to another group. An audience will listen to a vocally free, emotionally connected, clear thinking actor who intelligently and passionately expands into whatever vocal territory best suits the task of acting the play.

Although the concept of "good speech" for the stage is nothing new, it wasn't yet around in Shakespeare's time. Its ironic that Shakespeare, at the top of the heap of "classic texts," should be spoken in a style that neither reflects our own culture nor that of Elizabethan England. Rules of "good speech" would be repugnant to the actors and audience of Shakespeare's time.

> The period in which Shakespeare wrote was one of considerable linguistic freedom and experimentation...in some respects, [Shakespeare's pronunciation] was far more colloquial than might be considered proper or acceptable today...there

> is no record of the existence of stage pronunciation at that
> time...—Helge Kokeritz, *Shakespeare's Pronunciation*

It was actually a hundred years after Shakespeare's time that fastidious pronunciation became a cultural obsession:

> Eighteenth century London abounded with spelling masters
> and pronunciation coaches.... Common pronunciation...
> changed considerably during this period; partly through ordinary change, partly through the teaching of "correctness."
> ...the new standard was to a considerable extent...an artificial
> creation, based on false premises.—Raymond Williams, *The
> Long Revolution*

The artificial speech of the eighteenth century, the birth of "Elocution," and today's strict conventions for speaking "classic texts" seem to have little relationship to the aesthetic of Shakespeare's writing and the Elizabethan theater. Shakespeare never intended his work to sound so highbrow.

Here are some word pairs used as rhymes in Shakespeare's plays: cross-loss, crossed-engrossed, cost-boast, bob-crab, and doffed-craft.

It doesn't take a linguist to see that the vowel which in "Good Speech for Classic Texts" is recognized as / ɒ / was actually pronounced in a variety of ways in Shakespeare's time. Scholars find inconsistencies in Shakespeare's rhymes, and, of course, modern American speech is filled with inconsistencies as well. The difference is that today, we celebrate the inconsistencies *less*, and correct them *more*. Here are a few of the inconsistencies in American speech that get lost in the uniformity of "Good Speech for Classic Texts."

The Use of / ɒ / or / ɑ / in Short O Words

/ ɒ / has been called an "unstable" vowel, meaning that it isn't universally used in an American accent, and that one person might use it inconsistently in his/her accent. For instance you might hear the same person say NOT / nɒt / and GOD /gɑd /.

It seems unnecessarily limiting to say that / ɒ / is the "good" or preferred pronunciation of Short O words in "classic texts." Considering that Short O words were handled in a variety of ways in Shakespeare's time, there's no inherent aesthetic advantage in doing so. Today, some American use / ɒ / for Short O words, some use /ɑ /. Some mix it up and use / ɒ / and / ɑ / inconsistently. To deign one of these pronunciations better than the other artificially engineers the evolution of pronunciation in favor of one region or class.

The Use of / a / or / æ / in ASK Words

Another "unstable" vowel is / a / the Middle A. Some Americans use / a / for "ask" words; ask, laugh, path, class, grasp, dance, etc., but most use / æ /. In British speech "ask" words are pronounced with /ɑ /, as in /ask /; /laf /, /paθ /, /klas/,

/ grasp /, / dans /, etc. But in Elizabethan times these words were pronounced with the same short vowel as Short A words like: hat, pan, and crash.

The use or loss of "R Coloring"

One of the features of "Good American Speech," a.k.a. "Good Speech for Classic Texts," is the loss of "R" before a consonant or at the end of a word. FIRM, WARM, and CAR are to be pronounced as / fɜm /, / wɔm /, and / kɑ /. Again, this seems out of keeping with the aesthetic inherent in Shakespeare's writing. The plays cry out for a strong, lusty R!

Shakespeare's contemporary, Ben Jonson, said, "R is the dog's letter and hurreth in the sound." The word hurr means to trill, like the growl of a dog. Jonson goes on to describe the formation of R as "the tongue striking the inner palate, with trembling about the teeth. It is sounded firm in the beginning of the words, and more liquid in the middle and ends as in rarer, riper." Jonson defines a liquid sound as one that "melteth in the uttering...the tongue striking the roof of the palate gently." Jonson's description indicates a strong, distinctive R in all positions: beginning, medial, preconsonant, and final. R in all positions must have been part of Shakespeare's sound aesthetic; to eliminate the R in preconsonant and final positions, actually robs the speaker of the brilliance and sensuality of R. A strong R is a prevailing characteristic of American speech. In some accents, R has faded from a lusty, red-blooded sound to pale vestigial, neutrality. I'm not suggesting that if your native accent has a soft or dropped R that you do anything to change it, nor that you affect trilling your initial R. If however, you speak with a strong R, or a hard R, or any other kind of intelligible R that can be labeled and condemned, don't let yourself be talked out of it so easily.

The loss of "R coloring" in British speech may have been influenced by the Hanoverian rulers of England. In 1714 George I came to the throne from Germany without knowing a word of English. His son, George II who arrived in England at the age of seventeen as Prince of Wales, ascended to the throne with a command of the English language, and a German accent. His speech patterns and those of his German courtiers may have been a factor in the softening of the British R. This Germanic influence reaches into the nineteenth century and the reign of Victoria, who, as a child, learned to speak German before she learned to speak English. The softer British R would have had no resonance with the speech patterns of the Elizabethan and Jacobean stage.

Shakespeare's Speech

As an example of the colloquial way of speaking in Shakespeare's time, here is a reconstruction of the way Shakespeare's actors might have spoken, adapted from *Shakespeare's Pronunciation* by Helge Kokeritz, Yale University Press 1953. This transcription follows three points made by Kokeritz, concerning Shakespeare's pronunciation:

> 1. Shakespeare is thought to have spoken with a fully sounded R in both preconsonant and final positions. There was no uniform pronunciation

of R on the Elizabethan stage. The concept of standard speech for the stage did not exist in Shakespeare's time.

2. There is no vestige of evidence that /a / was deliberately used on the Elizabethan stage rather than the colloquial /æ /.

3. When Shakespeare first came to London he "undoubtedly" used /ɑ / rather than /ɒ / in Short O words such as HOT and STOP. And any assumption that he changed this sound to /ɒ/ would be based on "scanty, ambiguous evidence."

spɛːk   ðə spiːtʃ ɑɪ prɛː ju əz ɑɪ prəˈnəʊnst ɪt
Speak the speech, I pray you, as I pronounced it

tʊ ju ˈtrɪpn̩lɪ ɑn ðə tʌŋ   bət ɪf ju məʊð
to you, trippingly on the tongue. But if you mouth

ɪt əz mɛnɪ əv jər   ˈplɛːrz duː   əid   əz liːv
it, as many of your players do,   I would as leif

ðə təʊn ˈkrɑɪər spoːk mɪ ləɪnz nɔːr dʊ nat sɔː
the town cryer spoke my lines. Nor do not saw

ðə ɛːr tʊː mʌtʃ wɪð jər hænd ðʌs bət juːz
the air too much with your hand thus, but use

ɔːl ˈdʒɛntlɪ fər ɪn ðə vɛrɪ ˈtarənt ˈtɛmpɪst ænd əz
all gently, for in the very torrent, tempest, and, as

ɑɪ mɛː sɛː ðə ˈhwɜːrlwɪnd əv jər pæʃn̩ ju mʌst
I may say, the whirlwind of your passion, you must

əˈkwɑɪər ənd bɪˈgɪt ə ˈtɛmprəns   ðət mɛː gɪv ɪt
acquire and beget a temperance that may give it

ˈsmuːðnɪs   oː ɪt əˈfɛnz mɪ tə ðə soːl tʊ ɪːr
smoothness. O it offends me to the soul to hear

ə rəˈbʌstʃəs ˈpɛrɪwɪg ˈpɛːtɪd ˈfɛlo tɛːr ə ˈpæʃn̩ tə
a robustious periwig pated fellow tear a passion to

'tætərz tə 'vɛrɪ rægz tə splɪt ðə ɛ:rz ə ðə
tatters, to very rags, to split the ears of the

'grəʊnlɪnz hu: fər ðə mo:s part ər 'kɛ:pəbl əv
groundlings, who for the most part are capable of

no:θn̩ bət ɪnɛks'plɪkəbl̩ dʌm ʃo:zən̩neɪz əɪ
nothing but inexplicable dumb shows and noise. I

kʊd əv sʌtʃ ə 'felo hwɪpt fər o:r'du:ən
could have such a fellow whipped for o'erdoing

'ta:rməgənt ɪt əʊt 'hɛrədz 'hɛrəd prɛ: ju əvəɪd ɪt
Termagent. It out Herods Herod. Pray you avoid it.

bi: nat tʊ: tɛ:m 'nɛ:ðər bət lɛt jər o:n dɪs'krɛʃn
Be not too tame neither but let your own discretion

bɪ jər 'tjutər ʃu:t ðə 'ækʃn tə ðə w3:rd ðə
be your tutor. Suit the action to the word, the

w3:rd tə ðə ækʃn wɪð̩ðɪs spɛʃl əbz'a:rvəns ðət
word to the action, with this special observance that

ju o:rstɛp nat ðə 'madəstɪ əv nɛ:tər fər 'ɛnɪθɪŋ
you o'erstep not the modesty of nature. For anything

so: o:vər'dʌn ɪz fram ðə 'p3:rpəs əv 'plɛ:ən huz
so overdone is from the purpose of playing, whose

ɛnd bo:θ ət ðə f3:rst ən̩neʊ waz ən ɪz tʊ
end, both at the first and now, was and is, to

o:ld əs twɛ:r ðə 'mɪrər ʌp tə 'nɛ:tər tə ʃo:
hold as 'twere, the mirror up to nature. To show

'vɑːrtə ər oːn 'fɛːtər skɔːrn ər oːn 'ɪmɪʤ
virtue her own feature, scorn her own image,

ən ðə 'vɛrɪ ɛːʤ ən 'bɑdɪ ə ðə təɪm ɪz
and the very age and body of the time is

fɔːrm ən 'prɛsər nəʊ ðɪs oːvər'dʌn ər kʌm
form and pressure. Now this overdone, or come

'tɑːrdɪ ɔːf ðoː t mɛːk ð ʌns'kɪlfʊl læf
tardy off, though it make the unskillful laugh,

'kænɑt bət mɛːk ðə ʤu'dɪʃəs griːv ðə sɛnsər
cannot but make the judicious grieve, the censure

əv ðə hwɪtʃ oːn mʌst ɪn jʊr ə'ləʊns oːrwɛː
of the which one must, in your allowance, o'erweigh

ə hoːl 'θɪətər əv 'ʌðərz oː ðɛːr biː
a whole theater of others. O there be

'plɛːərz ðət əɪv siːn plɛː ən hɑːrd 'ʌðərz prɛːz
players that I've seen play, and heard others praise,

ən ðæt 'həɪlɪ nɑt̪tə spɛːk t prə'fɛːnlɪ ðæt
and that highly, not to speak it profanely, that

'nɛːðər ævn ðɪ 'æksənt əv 'krɪstʃənz nɔːr ðə
neither heaven, the accent of Christians, nor the

gɛːt əv 'krɪstʃən pɛːgən nɔːr mæn əv soː 'strʌtɪd
gait of Christian, Pagen, nor man, have so strutted

ən 'bɛlod ðət əɪv θɔːt sʌm əf 'nɛːtərz
and bellowed that I've thought some of nature's

'ʤ3:rnɪmən əd   mɛ:d   mɛn   ən   nɑt   mɛ:d   m̩

journeymen   had   made   men,   and   not   made   them

wɛl   ðɛ: ɪmɪ'tɛ:tɪd   hju'mænɪtɪ   so: ə'bɑmɪnəblɪ
well,   they   imitated   humanity   so   abominably.

Even in the largest theater, the relationship between actor and audience has a level of intimacy. An actor's live sound waves literally resonate in the bodies of the audience. Actors and audience share the same air. The atoms that comprise the air we breathe are as old as language. Each incoming breath contains atoms previously breathed not just by those around us, but potentially by any other person who ever lived. The laws of physics prove that there are atoms in our bodies right now that once fueled the voices of Shakespeare's actors:

Early Modern English, 1600

ɔ:l   ðə   w3:rldz   ə   stɛ:ʤ   ən   ɔ:l   ðə   mɛn   ən
"All   the   world's   a   stage   and   all   the   men   and

wɪmɪn   'mi:rlɪ   'plɛ:ərz
women   merely   players."

Middle English, 1375

Chaucer's own rendition of the Canterbury Tales:

hwan   ðat   'a:p'ɪl   wɪθ   ɪz   'ʃu:'əz   'so:tə   ðə   d'u:xt   əv
"Whan   that   Aprille   with   is   showres   soute   the   druxt   of

ma'rtʃ   aθ   'pɛ:'səd   to   ðə   'o:tə
March   hath   perced   to   the   rote."

Old English, 700 a.d.

And the first telling of the story of Beowulf:

hwæt   weɪ   'gardeɪnə   ɪn   'jeɪrdagʊm
"What   we   Gar-Dena   in   gèardagum

θeɪɔdkunɪngə   θrum   jɛ'frunɔn
thèodcyninga   thrym   gefrùnon

hu   θɑ   æð'ɛlɪngas   'ɛlɛn   'frɛmɛdɔn

hù   thà   æpelingas   ellen   fremedon..."

    Old English and Middle English ask for more energy from your mouth and the rest of your body than Modern English does. In Middle English, two words for the chest were soundhoard and wordhoard—suggesting a below-the-neck experience of language. Couragé, a Middle English word for the heart, suggests that emotions live in the body as well. As you speak in these older forms of English, what do you notice? Could you imagine talking with this much energy all the time? Let these words and phrases stimulate your senses and appetites. Can you bring some of the richness of these languages into the Modern English you speak? I'm not suggesting that you alter your accent by mimicking antiquated sound patterns, but that you take a new, more energetic approach to your own accent and your own tongue. Perhaps by rerooting yourself in these earlier incarnations of English you can open the door to a more sensual and visceral approach to the language you speak.

    Just think, with every breath atoms enter and leave the body at the rate of ten to the twenty-second power. An outgoing breath expels atom-sized bits of waste from every part of the body. The breath you speak with today will someday be mingled into the breath of people of different accents and languages, different places, different times.

Part Four
Accents

>...How many ages hence
>Shall this our lofty scene be acted o'er
>In states unborn and accents yet unknown?
>—William Shakespeare, *Julius Caesar*

This isn't a course in stage accents. There are already many such resources available. If you need to learn an accent quickly, I suggest you go to one of them. Instead, this is a way to develop the skills for creating stage accents on your own and refining accents that you've already learned.

You'll learn accents by listening to native speakers, transcribing the sounds that you hear, playing pillow games in order to feel the sounds in your body, and working on a play. Sometimes actors wait too long to incorporate accents into rehearsal, either because they're having difficulty learning the accent, or, feel it will in some way interfere with the early rehearsal process.

In my experience coaching actors, they're sometimes fine at practicing the sound changes in isolation, but lose the accent once they really start acting. I suggest that you bring the accent to rehearsal as early as possible. Make your embodiment of the accent part and parcel of your embodiment of the words of the play.

However, don't limit your practice of the accent to the words of the play only. Speak with the accent all the time for awhile. Integrate it into your daily routine. Take it with you on your errands. Let it become a living, breathing part of you.

The accent work here is supplemental to the research and imaginative homework of embodying the life and ways of other cultures. Acting in an accent requires your body's deep acceptance of new ways of saying words— thinking and breathing in an accent is just as important as speaking in it. To know an accent is to know a region's climate and topography, a person's cultural heritage and family background.

The games with phonetic pillows in this section will help you ground each new accent in your body. As you play with the pillows remember that vibrations love attention. Imagine that you are seeing and feeling the sounds of accents as well as hearing them. Watch them cover distance as you fling them around the room. As you explore accents you're exploring new frontiers and facets of your own voice. Your body becomes a tuning fork for the expression of the voices of the people of other cultures.

Pronunciation Contrasts

By training your ear to hear the subtle nuances of your own pronunciation, you will increase your ability to identify, analyze, and assimilate the accents of other people.

The following exercises will help you identify the features of your own accent and the accents of others. You will contrast pronunciations, tune your body to unfamiliar sounds, and do scene work in different accents.

I say /pə'teɪto/  I say /pə'tɑto/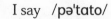

This is a pronunciation contrast. A pronunciation contrast compares two pronunciations of the same word. There is for instance, a contrast between a British and U.S. pronunciation of the word ASK.

A big part of learning an accent is discovering how it contrasts with your own accent. So before studying other accents it's necessary for you to examine the way you form sounds yourself. Once you understand your own accent, you can determine the sound shifts needed to speak in another accent.

Personal Accent Inventory

Let's begin with something very personal, your name. The way you say your name is completely up to you. Your identity is tuned to its vibrations. Other people may say your name differently from you, but your way can't be wrong—after all, it's *your* name. Maybe you go by a few different names. For instance, my name is Louis, but some people call me Lou or Louie; I pronounce my Italian last name in a decidedly New Jersey way.

In Italian, the spelling of my name sounds out as CO LAI AN NI which could be transcribed in the IPA as /kolaɪ'ɑnˌni /. In Italian a double N indicates holding on to the N sound longer; AI together form a diphthong similar to a U.S. pronunciation of the word EYE / aɪ /, the second A has the open sound of a Broad A / ɑ /, and the final I is pronounced with the long vowel / i /.

In New Jersey, the double N is reduced to a short sound, the diphthong / aɪ / is replaced with / i /, and the second A turns to / ɛə / (as the vowel in the word AIR). The New Jersey pronunciation could be transcribed phonetically as /koli'ɛəni /. You can see that this pronunciation doesn't fit very well with the spelling—still it's *my* name, and that's the way I say it. Consider this example when analyzing the sounds of your own name:

Say your name fully (and any variations you use) out loud.

How would you write this phonetically? Is it the same way other people say your name or is there a contrast?

Listen to several other people say your name. This is tricky because you don't want them to listen and repeat it the way you say it. Prompt them to say it without saying it yourself. Transcribe their pronunciations—just as you hear them.

How do your parents say your name? Grandparents? Brothers and sisters? Other relatives? If they're not around, let your memory tell you. Do any of their pronunciations contrast with your own? How would you transcribe them?

How do your teachers, classmates, and friends say your name? Transcribe these, too.

Try comparing other pronunciations such as the name of your hometown, other family names, expressions you use, etc.

Ear Training

In order to compare the sounds of your accent to someone else's, you've got to listen for more than just vowel and consonant changes. As you work with a partner, you may find that you both transcribe a sound with the same symbol yet there is something different about the way each of you says it. In order to express these subtle differences in transcription, you will need more than just phonetic symbols. Theoretically, there may be an absolute /i /, /u / , or /ɑ / , but in practice, every single person makes sounds a little differently. The indefinite gray area between the fixed sounds of the phonetic alphabet is where most language actually happens.

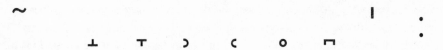

These are called "diacritical markings." They can help you to identify the nuance of the way someone speaks. The word diacritical has a rather clinical, detached sound. Because diacritical markings detail the nuance of the way someone speaks, I prefer to call them "nuance markings." Throughout the text diacritical markings will be referred to as nuance markings. It should be noted that there is room for creativity in the use of nuance markings. It has been acknowledged by the International Phonetic Alphabet Association that the IPA does not provide the full spectrum of markings necessary to accurately set down the pronunciation characteristics of all accents. As Roe-Merrill S. Heffner says in the book *General Phonetics*, "If special symbols are required they can be selected and defined when used." For this reason the nuance markings used here may differ from those that you have encountered in other texts.

If a sound is extra NASAL, you can draw a squiggle / ˜/ above the symbol, like this, / ĩ / .

Say these words with the extra nasality indicated: PLEASE, / plĩz /, THAT, / ðæ̃t /, FATHER, / fɑ̃ðɚ /, NOW, / nɑ̃ʊ /.

If a vowel is elongated, put a colon after the symbol, like this, / : /.

Say these vowels with extra elongation, /i: / , / ɑ: / , / ɔ: / , / ɛ: /.

To indicate a different tongue position for the same sound, you can use these markings: / ̣ / means the tongue position is higher; / ̢ / means the tongue position is lower. If the word PEN almost sounds like PIN, but the tongue doesn't go quite as high as the / ɪ / position, use / ̣ /—the tongue raising mark—/ pẹn /. If the word SIT sounds almost like SET, but the tongue isn't quite as low as / ɛ /, use / ̢ /—the tongue lowering mark—/ sɛ̢t /.

Make these sounds with your tongue lower than its position in the *habitual* formation of each, /i̢/, /æ̢/, /ɑ̢/, /o̢/, /ɔ̢/, /ʊ̢/, /u̢/

Make these sounds with the tongue higher than its position in the *habitual* formation of each, /ị/, /æ̣/, /ɑ̣/, /ọ/, /ɔ̣/, /ʊ̣/, /ụ/

If a sound is made with extra LIP ROUNDING it can be transcribed with this marking under it / ̜ /. For instance, if the word MOON is said with very rounded lips it can be transcribed as / mu̜n /.

If a sound is made with extra LIP STRETCHING, it can be transcribed with this marking under it / ̜ /. The word SEE with extra lip stretching can be transcribed as /si̜ /.

Say these words with extra LIP ROUNDING: WHO / hu̜ /, DON'T /do̜ʊnt / SAW / sɔ̜ /.

Say these words with extra LIP STRETCHING: HE / hi̜ /, LATE / lɛ̜ɪt /, ASK / æ̜sk /.

If a voiced consonant is pronounced without voice, it is called "devoiced." Devoiced sounds can be transcribed with this marking underneath them / ̥ /. A devoiced "b" transcribed this way, / b̥/, sounds more like "p."

Say these words with devoiced consonants where indicated: THESE /ð̥i̥z̥ /, DRIVE /d̥raɪv̥/, EDGE , /ɛd̥ʒ /.

Depending on the accent, a voiced consonant may be completely, or only partially, devoiced. Try different degrees of devoicing. If you partially devoice /b/ for instance, it softens and becomes more breathy, but it doesn't completely lose its identity and become / p /, it just goes toward /p /.

If the teeth are used in place of another articulating surface, for instance, if / d / is made between the top front teeth and the tongue rather than the gum ridge and the tongue, it's called a "dental" sound and can be transcribed with this marking / ̪ / beneath it / d̪/.

Say these words using dental consonants: DAY / d̪ei /, TO / t̪u /, NOW / n̪aʊ /, LOW / l̪oʊ /.

If a consonant (particularly / l /, / m / or / n /) is used as an entire syllable, it is called a "syllabic" consonant and can be transcribed with a dot underneath it, like this, /m̩ /, / l̩ /, / n̩ / in words like SPASM / 'spæzm̩/, LITTLE / 'lɪtl̩ /, and WOODEN /'wʊdn̩ /.

Accented syllables can be noted with this marking / ' / placed in front of the first sound in the accented syllable, as in these words, HELLO / 'hə'loʊ /, UNDER /'ʌndɚ / AWAY / ə'weɪ /.

Nuance Markings and Inventing Language

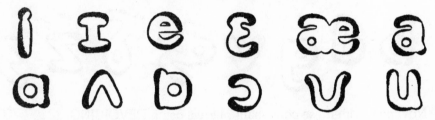

Now that you're familiar with all the markings, use the vowel pillows illustrated above in several rounds of the "Inventing Language" game—see page 43. In round one of "Inventing Language" use extra NASALITY for all sounds. Notice if all this nasality has any affect on the game:

> Is your body moved differently?
> How do you feel?
> How do you relate to other people and their sounds?
> Does releasing sound in this way feel familiar?
> Does it feel quite foreign?

After playing the game for a while, come back to speaking words; either say a monologue, read one of the scenes from the play, or just have a conversation with someone. As you speak, retain the extra nasality of the vowels.

> Whom do you know that speaks this way?
> Are you reminded of any accent?
> Is your body convinced that honest communication is possible with this kind of sound?

Round Two
Continue with the vowel pillows as above, but this time experiment with ELONGATING the sounds as you play the game. Go through the same steps and ask yourself the same questions as you did with NASALITY.

Round Three
Continue the game as above, this time with your TONGUE RAISED higher for each sound than your usual formation.

Round Four
This time play the game with your TONGUE LOWER than its usual position for each sound.

Round Five
This time play the game with more LIP ROUNDING.

Round Six
This time with more LIP STRETCHING.

Now play with these consonant pillows using DEVOICING.

Play with these consonant pillows using DENTALIZING.

Now that your body has explored all of these "diacritical" nuances, read scenes from the plays that lend themselves to these adjustments. For instance, you could try scene / ɔ / with extra LIP ROUNDING, scene / i / with extra ELONGATION, scene / d / with DENTALIZING, and scene / ð / with DEVOICING.

Also try reading the FRENCH SCENES using extra nasality and changing the accented syllables of words.

Now take the nuance markings and any new awareness into your work on pronunciation contrasts and accents.

Additional Nuance Markings
If there is extra breathiness in a vowel, it can be transcribed with this symbol beneath it /   /. An extra breathy / ɑ / would be transcribed as / ɑ̈ /.

If a plosive consonant is aspirated it can be marked with this symbol following it / ʰ /. An aspirated / p / would be transcribed as / pʰ /. If a consonant is formed but not released, it can be marked with this symbol after it / ˌ /. An unreleased / t / would be transcribed as / tˌ /.

In addition to the marks for tongue raising / ˔ / and tongue lowering / ˕ /, there are also marks for the tongue being further back / ˗ / and further forward / ˖ /. And in addition to the nuance mark for devoicing of voiced consonants / ˳ /, there is a mark for voicing of voiceless consonants, / ˬ /. A voiced / t / would sound more like / d / and would be transcribed as / tˬ /.

Variants in Vowel Pronunication

Each of these words has more than one common pronunciation. Say each word out loud and see if any of the transcriptions match your pronunciation. If not, add the transcription of your pronunciation to the list and compare to the others.

Variants in Vowel Pronunciation

Word	Some Common Pronunciations
feel	fil fɪl fɪəl fəl
been	bɪn bɛn bɪən bɛən
pen	pɛn pɪn pɪən pɛən
stale	stɛəl steɪl stɛl
where	hwɛɚ hwɛr hwær wɛɚ
ran	ræn rɛən rɛn
cattle	'kætl 'kædl 'kɛdl
had	hæd hɛd ˈhɛəd˙
ant	ænt ɛənt ɛnt iənt
cast	kæst kɛəst kast
aunt	ænt ɑnt ɛənt ant ɔnt
can't	kænt kɛnt kɛənt kant
just	dʒʌst dʒɪst dʒɛst
hot	hɑt hɒt hat
spot	spɑt spɒt spat
lava	lɑvə lævə lɒvə
law	lɔ lɑ lɒ
bought	bɔt bat bɒt
caught	kɔt kat kɒt kʌt
go	goʊ go gəʊ
most	moʊst most məʊst
stood	stʊd stʌd
full	fʊl fʌl
roof	ruf rʊf rʌf
eye	aɪ ɑɪ ɒɪ ʌɪ
tie	taɪ tɑɪ tɒɪ tʌɪ
pipe	paɪp pɑɪp pɒɪp pʌɪp
blind	blaɪnd blɑɪnd blɒɪnd blʌɪnd
ounce	aʊns æʊns ɛəʊns ɑʊns
town	taʊn tæʊn tɛəʊn tɑʊn
flour	flaʊɚ flaʊr flɑʊɚ
boil	bɔɪl bɒɪl buil bɔl
voice	vɔɪs vɒɪs vuis vɔs
joy	dʒɔi dʒɑɪ dʒui dʒɔ
due	du dju
Tuesday	'tuzdeɪ 'tuzdi 'tjuzdɪ

suit	sut sjut
strength	strɛnθ strɪŋθ strɛnθ
water	ˈwɔtɚ ˈwʊdɚ ˈwadɚ
Monday	ˈmʌndeɪ ˈmʌndɪ
Christmas	ˈkrismɪs ˈkrɪsməs
drama	dramə ʤramə dræmə
theater	ˈθiətɚ ˈθidɚ θiˈeɪdɚ
foyer	ˈfɔɪɚ fɔɪˈeɪ
again	əˈgɛn əˈgɪn əˈgeɪn
either	ˈiðɚ ˈaɪðɚ
neither	ˈniðɚ ˈnaɪðɚ
tomato	təˈmeɪto təˈmato
piano	piˈæno ˈpjæno ˈpjano piˈɛəno
resort	rɪˈzɔ˞t ˈrizɔ˞t
February	ˈfɛbruɛ˞ɪ ˈfɛbjuɛ˞ɪ
bury	ˈbɛrɪ ˈbɛri ˈbʌri ˈbɝi
creek	krik krɪk
marry	mærɪ mɛɚɪ
Mary	mɛɚɪ mɛrɪ
merry	mɛrɪ mɛɚɪ mɝɪ
orange	ˈɔɚɪnʤ arnʤ ɔrnʤ
stomach	ˈstʌmɪk ˈstʌmək
humor	ˈhjumɚ ˈjumɚ
greasy	ˈgrisɪ ˈgrizi ˈgrisi
this	ðɪs dɪs
which	hwɪtʃ wɪtʃ
Detroit	diˈtrɔɪt ˈditrɔɪt
Arkansas	ˈarkɪnsɔ arˈkænzɪs
Missouri	mɪˈzɝə məˈzuri
Florida	ˈflɔrɪdə ˈflarɪdə

How do you say the vowels in these words? How do other people say them? What other word pairs (or sound pairs) can you add to the list that will help you identify pronunciation contrasts?

FEEL	FILL	FAIL	FELL
HE'LL	HILL	SAIL	SELL
DEAL	DILL	TAIL	TELL
PIN	PEN	PAIN	PEN
WIN	WHEN	YAWN	YON
BEEN	BEN	CAUGHT	COT
SHELL	SHALL	KETTLE	CATTLE
BEG	BAG	POOL	PULL
MEN	MAN	WHO'D	HOOD
HEAD	HAD	LUKE	LOOK
KEN	CAN	BUCK	BOOK

LUCK	LOOK	JUST	GIST
UPS	OOPS	MUST	MIST
HUD	HOOD	FUN	FIN
STUD	STOOD	LUMP	LIMP
BALL	BOIL	BOAT	BOUGHT
JAW	JOY	NODE	GNAWED
GNAWS	NOISE	COAL	CALL
ROOF	ROUGH	TOWN	TAN
ROOM	RUM	LOUD	LAD
SPAT	SPOT	HOUND	HAND
CAT	COT	PIPE	PAP
HAT	HOT	BLIND	BLAND
LACK	LOCK	FIGHT	FAT
TAP	TOP	PIPE	POP
HOLE	HALL	KIND	CONNED
LOW	LAW	LIGHT	LOT
PLAYED	PLEAD	AUNT	ANT
TRAY	TREE	KEPT	CAPPED
LAKE	LEAK	PEDDLE	PADDLE
DO	DUE	SUCK	SOCK
LOOT	LUTE	LUCK	LOCK
TOON	TUNE	GUT	GOT
TIE	TOY	CASED	CAST
FILE	FOIL	CLAIM	CLAM
VICE	VOICE	PACE	PASS
OAT	OUT	WREN	RUN
LOAD	LOUD	DECK	DUCK
KNOWN	NOUN	REST	RUST
BOAT	BOUT	STALK	STUCK
EYE	AH	DAWN	DONE
SPY	SPA	COST	CUSSED
PINED	POND	CAP	CUP
LATE	LET	RAPTURE	RUPTURE
DALE	DELL	HASSLE	HUSTLE
RAIN	WREN	HAG	HUG
WAN	ONE	BAG	BUG
CALM	COME	SADDLE	SUBTLE

How do you say these consonants? How do other people say them? What word pairs can you add to this list that will help you to identify pronunciation contrasts?

WITCH	WHICH	SHAKING	SHAKEN
WEAL	WHEEL	ROTTING	ROTTEN
WIT	WHIT	RINGING	RIGGING
TAKING	TAKEN	SANG	SAG

BANGER	BAGGER	THINK	FINK
HUNG	HUN	EITHER	ETHER
LONG	LAWN	TEETHE	TEETH
RANG	RAN	THY	THIGH
TOLL	TOLD	TANK	THANK
SOLE	SOLD	TIN	THIN
PACKED	PACK	EATER	ETHER
ASKED	ASK	THOSE	DOZE
HAD	HAT	THEN	DEN
SAID	SET	HEATHER	HEADER
DEAR	TIER	SUE	ZOO
MEASURE	MESHER	PACE	PAYS
AZURE	ASHER	DOSE	DOZE
PAST	PASS	FUSSY	FUZZY
CURSED	CURSE	THINK	SINK
WORSE	WORST	THIN	SIN
TAP	TAB	THICK	SICK
POOR	BOOR	SHINGLE	SINGLE
STAPLE	STABLE	SHILL	SILL
CHOOSE	SHOES	MESH	MESS
CHEESE	SHE'S	PINE	FINE
ETCHER	ESCHER	PILL	FILL
LEACH	LEASH	PORT	FORT
SEAT	SHEET	BIRD	BUD
CENSOR	CENSURE	SEARCH	SUCH
SWISS	SWISH	LURK	LUCK
SEIZE	SEETHE	HER	HEH
BREEZE	BREATHE	HEARD	HEAD
TEASE	TEETHE	BIRD	BED
CAB	GAB	SHIRRED	SHOULD
TRICKER	TRIGGER	TURK	TOOK
BACK	BAG	BEARING	BEDDING
RED	WED	HERRING	HEADING
ARRAY	AWAY	EARRING	EATING
ORE	AWE	JARRING	JOTTING
FAIL	VALE	DECEIVE	RECEIVE
LEAF	LEAVE	DEFILE	REFILE
RIFLE	RIVAL		

How do you say these final consonant words?

OATH	OAF	BACON	BAKING
DEATH	DEAF	EATEN	EATING
MYTH	MIFF	SOOTH	SOOTHE
WREATH	REEF	LOOSE	LOSE
SHEATH	SHEAF	NOOSE	NEWS
GARDEN	GUARDING	RACE	RAISE

Do you pronounce the R in these words?

LOVER	LOVE A
LEAR	LEAH
AIR	(Y)EAH
SPAR	SPA
SOAR	SAW
SIRE	SIGH A
EMPLOYER	EMPLOY A
ENDOWER	ENDOW A

Do you attach these linking consonants to the first or second word?

GLOBE OLD	GLOW BOLD
BREAK UP	BRAY CUP
LOAD IN	LOW DIN
LIFE IS	LYE FIZZ
HAIG ATE	HAY GATE
SEEK ANDY	SEE CANDY
ALL OUT	AWE LOUT
SEEM OTHER	SEE MOTHER
AN OAT	A NOTE
CAPE ANN	KAY PAN
KEEP IN	KEY PIN
SOAR OVER	SAW ROVER
FORCE ED	FORE SAID
DRIVE AT	DRY VAT
GO UNDER	GO WONDER
RAY'S OWN	RAY ZONE

The Classroom as an Accent Lab

Having compared your own accent to the accents of others, you can now begin to apply your skills to the creation of stage accents. First, you need to locate people with the accents you want to learn; for lack of a better word, accent "donors" (this is the term Jerry Blunt used in *Stage Dialects*, 1967.) The word donor seems a little severe, as if you're asking for blood rather than help with an accent. However, I like it because it reminds me that a person who shares their accent with me is sharing a vital part of themselves. I am the recipient of a part of this person and they are indeed the donor.

If you're at a universtiy you might begin your search for a donor at the office of international student affairs. You could also try the English as a Second Language (ESL) department on campus, or a private language school.

Accent donors may be willing to swap a few hours of taping and interviewing for some help with English pronunciation, or a ticket to your next production. The classroom can become an accent lab; students can share the accents they learn outside of class, and people with accents can visit the class as donors. There is potential for researching and learning many accents within the time of a single course.

Outlining an Accent

You now have the tools to begin learning accents. Below is a sample chart which shows how to outline the accents of your donors. In this chart I have compared key word pronunciations of my own accent to those of my donors. In the column to the left I have placed the phonetic symbols. In the next column, beside the corresponding symbol, I have entered a key work and its transcription in my own accent. In the next four columns I have transcribed each key work into the accents of my donors. I arrived at these transcriptions by listening to my donors—each are native speakers from the country indicated—conversing and reading scenes from the phonetically-driven plays in the back of the book. I selected the strongest and most consistent sound shifts present in the accent of each donor. When necessary, I used nuance markings to indicate subtleties of pronunciation such as elongation, lip rounding or stretching, tongue raising or lowering, voicing of voiceless consonants, devoicing of voiced sounds, nasality, breathiness, extra aspiration, unreleased sounds, and dentalization.

I have included the unstable vowels / a /, / ɒ /, and / ju / (for words like NEW, DUKE, SUIT, TUNE, LUNAR) in the outline chart. For although they do not occur in my own accent, they often occur in the accents of donors.

Here is some background information on each of the donors whose accents are outlined in the chart.

French Accent

Bernard (pronounced / bɛəˈnɑˈʔ / is forty-five years old and has lived in the U.S. for several years. In France he had worked as a policeman and a racecar driver. He now teaches at a small liberal arts college. His accent is typically Parisian. Notice the nasality marks in the french accent transcriptions. Nasality will be indicated by a squiggle above the affected sound. For instance, the word DEMANDS is transcribed as / dɪmɑ̃z /. In a French accent, vowels followed by / m / or / n / are usually nasal. The R in a French accent is formed between the soft palate and the back of the tongue in a uvular trill, which also resonates nasally. It is transcribed as / ʳ /. The word ROSE is transcribed as / ʳoz /. In the rhythm of the French accent, listen for unexpected accentuation in words such as ÁFFAIR, ÁBOUT, BÉFORE, CÁREER, NÉCESSITY, and CHROMÓSOMES.

German Accent

Brigette is a twenty-two year old university student. She came to the U.S. from Germany two months ago. She is studying business administration, but is mainly interested in improving her English. After a year in America, she plans to return to her native Augsberg to finish her degree. In a German accent, listen for extra breathiness in the sound of vowels. The nuance mark for breathiness is / ̤ /. In German, as in French, the R is formed between the soft palate and the back of the tongue. But rather than being nasal, it is breathy, especially at the beginning of a word. It will be transcribed with the symbol / ʳ /. Also listen for voiced consonants being partially devoiced. This makes them softer and, again, more breathy, but not whispered.

British Accent

David is a musician and conductor with the meticulous speaking style of those who have attended British public boarding school. Although originally from Yorkshire, his accent could be characterized as British RP (see page 52.) I have used the nuance mark / ˌ / to denote the extra lip rounding of the vowel / ɔ /, and the mark / ˌ / to denote a high tongue position in the formation of the vowel / æ /.

Kenyan Accent

Joseph is from Kenya. He is twenty-seven and has been in the U.S. for six years. From childhood, he spoke English in school and a mixture of Swahili and his mother tongue Kikuyu / jɛˈkɔjʉ / at home. He is currently teaching mathematics while completing his PhD. Joseph speaks in a quiet, creaky voice which is sometimes difficult to hear. Frequent glottal stops between words give his speech a stacatto, halting rhythm. Words beginning with W and Y are sometimes pronounced with / ʔ / for example WOULD / ʔʊd / and YEAR / ʔɪə /. Some features of the Kenyan accent are similar to those of an American southern accent, for instance, shortening the dipthong / aɪ / to / ɑ /, and using / ʌ / in place of / ɝ /. The Kenyan R is made with a tap trill at the beginning of words and between vowels; the tip of the tongue touches the gum ridge forming something like a small d sound. The tap trill will be transcribed as / ʳ /. Before consonants and at the ends of words, R is dropped as in a British accent. In the Kenyan accent, the nuance marks for lip rounding / ˌ /, tongue raising / ˌ /, tongue lowering / ˌ /, tongue backing / ˍ /, aspirating / ʰ /, unreleased consonants / ˌ /, and dentalizing / ˌ / are used. Aside from sound shifts, the lilt of the Kenyan accent is very important. To the American ear it sounds somewhat monotone, but with sudden upward spikes in pitch and volume.

If you've ever tried to learn an accent from written transcription without hearing it, you'll realize how valuable it is to find a donor. Although you won't actually be able to learn the accents below simply by reading the donor outlines, you can use this chart as a guide to what to listen for when analyzing the accents of French, German, British, and Kenyan speakers. You'll find that there are no absolutes—pronunciations will differ somewhat from person to person and should be transcribed according to *your* ear, guided by your needs and tastes, not mine.

After familiarizing yourself with the outlines in this chart, seek out people who have these accents. Listen to them in conversation. Listen to them read the word lists and examples of sound shifts given in this chapter. Determine the strongest features in their accents, then have them read the scenes from the plays which correspond to those sound shifts. In addition to the general scenes, have the German donor read the German scenes, the French donor read the French scenes, and the British and Kenyan donors read the scene of special pronunciations.

It is important when creating your own accent outline charts that you begin with key word transcriptions of your own accent. This will enable you to approach phonetics from the point of view of your own pronunciations rather than the "standard" pronunciations of a ready-made chart.

Phonetic Symbol	Key Word List	Outline of Donor Pronunciation Contrasts			
Vowels	My Accent	Bernard France	Briggette Germany	David England (RP)	Joseph Kenya
i	MEAL mil	mĩl	mi̪l	mil	mi̪l
ɪ	HIP hɪp	ip	hɪ̪p	hɪp	hi̪p
eɪ	THEY ðeɪ	ze	g̊ e̪:	ðeɪ	d̥e:
ɛ	GET gɛt	get	gę̊t	gɛt	ge:t
æ	CRAB kræb	kʳæb	kʳɛ̪b	kræb	kʳab
æ, a, or ɑ In words like ask, path, cast.	BASK bæsk	bas̺k	b̥as̪k	bɑsk	bɑsk
ə	AGREE əˈgri	ˈəgʳi	̥əgʳi̪	əˈgri	əgʳi̪
ʌ	FUDGE fʌʤ	fʌʒ	fa̪ʤ	fʌʤ	faʤ
ɑ	SPA spɑ	spa	spʰɑ̪	spɑ	spʰa
ɚ	DINNER ˈdɪnɚ	ˈdinəʳ	ˈdɪ̪nəʳ	ˈdɪnə	ˈdi̪nə
ɝ	JERK ʤɝk	ʒɝʳk	ʤɝ̪ʳk	ʤɜːk	ʤʌk
ɑ or ɒ In words spelled with O or WA like odd, top, wash.	NOD nɑd	nʌd	nɒ̪d̪	nɒd	nɔd
ɔ	BOUGHT bɔt	bot	b̥ɔ̪t	bɔːt	bɔt
oʊ	KNOWN noʊn	nõn	no̪n	nəʊn	nọn
ʊ	GOOD gʊd	gud	gů̪d̪	gʊd	gu̪d
u	TRUE tru	tʳu̪	tʳu̪	tru	tʳu̪
aɪ	MIME maɪm	maĩm	ma̪ɪm	maɪm	mɑm
ɔɪ	CHOICE tʃɔɪs	ʃɔis	tʃɔ̪ɪ̪s̪	tʃɔɪs	tʃoɪs
aʊ	HOW haʊ	ãʊ	ha̪ʊ	haʊ	ho:
u or ju In words like suit, duke, new.	SUIT sjut	sut	s̪u̪t	sjut	sju̪t

Phonetic Symbol	Key Word List	Outline of Donor Pronunciation Contrasts			
R Dipthongs	My Accent	Bernard France	Briggette Germany	David England (RP)	Joseph Kenya
ɪɚ	HEAR hɪɚ	iəʳ	hiəʳ	hɪə	hiə
ɛɚ	CHAIR tʃɛɚ	ʃɛʳ	tʃɛəʳ	tʃɛə	tʃeə
ɑɚ	CARD kɑɚd	kɑʳd	kɑʳd̪	kɑːd	kɑːd
ɔɚ	PORK pɔɚk	poʳk	pɔ̣ʳk	pɔːk	pɔk
aɪɚ	TIRE taɪɚ	'taɪəʳ	tɑɪəʳ	taɪə	'taə
ɔɪɚ	LAWYER lɔɪɚ	'loːjəʳ	lɔɪəʳ	lɔɪə	'lɔɪə
aʊɚ	SCOUR skaʊɚ	'skaʊəʳ	'skaʊəʳ	'skaʊə	'skʰoːə
ʊɚ	POOR pʊɚ	pʊəʳ	puəʳ	pʊə	pʊ̯ə

Phonetic Symbol	Key Word List	Outline of Donor Pronunciation Contrasts			
Conso-nants	My Accent	Bernard France	Briggette Germany	David England (RP)	Joseph Kenya
b	BIB bɪb	bɪb	b̩ɪb̩	bɪb	bɪ̣b
p	TRAPPED træpt	tʳæpt	tʳɛ̣pʰt	træpt	tʳɑpʰt
d	DARED dɛɚd	dɛəʳd	d̪ɛ̣əʳd̪	dɛəd	d̪ɛəʳd̪
t	CATS kæts	kãts	kɛ̣t̪s̪	kæts	katʰs
v	VERVE vɝv	vɝʳv	v̥ɝʳv̥	vɝːv	vʌv̥
f	FIVE faɪv	faɪv	f̣ɑɪv̥	faɪv	fav̥
g	GAG gæg	gãg	g̥ɛ̣g̥	gæg	gɑg̥
k	SKILL skɪl	skɪl	skʰɪ̣l	skɪl	skʰɪ̣ ḷ
ð	THOSE ðoʊz	zoz	ð̥o̥z	ðəʊz	d̪o̥z
θ	THING θɪŋ	sĩŋ	sɪ̣ŋ	θɪŋ	θ̥ɪ̣ŋ

Phonetic Symbol	Key Word List	Outline of Donor Pronunciation Contrasts			
Consonants Continued	My Accent	Bernard France	Briggette Germany	David England (RP)	Joseph Kenya
dʒ	JUDGE	dʒʌdʒ	ʒʌʒ	dʒ̣ɑ̣dʒ	dʒʌdʒ	dʒɑdʒ
tʃ	CHILL	tʃɪl	ʃil	tʃɪ̣l	tʃɪl	tʃi̜ l̩
z	OZONE	'oʊzon	'ozõn	'o̜zon	'əʊzəʊn	'o:z̧ən
s	SOUND	saʊnd	saũnd	şɑʊnd̩	saʊnd	saʊnd̩
ʒ	MEASURE	'mɛʒɚ	'meʒəʳ	'mɛ̝ʒ̊əʳ	'mɛʒə	me:ʒəʳ
ʃ	SHAPE	ʃeɪp	ʃep	ʃeɪp	ʃeɪp	ʃe:pʰ
ŋ	GONG	gɑŋ	gʌ̃ŋ	g̊ɑ̣ŋk	gɒŋ	gɔŋ
m	MAP	mæp	mãæp	mɛ̝p	mæp	mɑp
n	NEW	nu	nũ	nu̜	nju	nu
l	LOSE	luz	lu̜z	lu̜z̧	luz	l̩ uz̧
r	ROSE	roʊz	ʳoz	ʳo̜z̧	rəʊz	ʳʳo:z
w	WAY	weɪ	we	ve̝:	weɪ	ʔʊe:
h	HOTEL	ho'tɛl	'otel	ho̜'tɛl	həʊ'tɛl	ho:'te:l̩
hw	WHICH	hwɪtʃ	hwiʃ	v̝ɪ̣tʃ	hwɪtʃ	hwi̝tʃ
j	YEAR	jiɚ	jiəʳ	jɪ̣əʳ	jɪə	iəʳ

You can also make a chart for consonant combinations in which there are pronunciation contrasts; for instance, some German speakers pronounce S as / ʃ / when it is in combination with T or K, as in the word STILL / ʃtɪl /.

Go through the consonant combinations to determine whether any pronunciation contrasts of this type occur in your donor's accent.

Checklist for Making an Accent Outline

When making accent outlines like those above, it will be helpful to use the following questions and word lists (as well as the plays in the back of the book) to identify sound shifts in an accent. When you have identified all the sound shifts, you can select those which most strongly suggest the accent and which will be most intelligible to the audience.

Since accents aren't sound changes alone, you'll need to figure out the LILT of the accent as well (see page 96).

Background Information

What is the donor's native country? For example; a Spanish accent from Spain will sound very different from a Spanish accent from Mexico.

What is the donor's native language? I have often been surprised to learn that someone with a heavy foreign accent has English as their native language!

How long have they been in the United States? What influence has the American accent had on them, if any?

Which is their primary language; English or their native language? Many people continue speaking their native language in the home, the community, and at work although living in America. Others seldom get a chance to speak their native language. Either circumstance will have an effect on their accent.

Where did they learn English and what was the accent of the person who taught them? Do they speak English with traces of a British accent, an American accent, or some other type of English-speaking accent?

How are their reading and writing skills? Their rate of literacy in English (and perhaps in their own language) will affect their grammar, vocabulary, and ability to sound-out words.

Sound Contrasts

Do they distinguish long vowel sounds from short vowel sounds in words like these?

/ it /	eat	/ ɪt /	it
/geɪt /	gate	/gɛt /	get
/kɑm/	calm	/kæm /	cam
/ ʃud /	shoed	/ ʃʊd /	should

Do they say the vowel in words such as pass, ask, bath, aunt, rather, dance, staff, laugh—with / æ / or with /ɑ / or some other vowel?

Do they say the vowel in words such as hot, bother, pop, knob, modern, bog, wash, what, or of with /ɑ / or with /ɒ / or some other vowel?

Do they say the vowel in words such as tube, suit, duty, lunar, stupid, new, cute, beauty, view, or Hubert with /u / or with /ju / or some other vowel?

How do they say R?

Do they use a "hard R" as in a Texas accent?

Do they ever "tap" an R, as in a Southern British pronunciation of VERY, / ˈvɛˈɪ /?

Do they ever "burr" an R as in a Scots pronunciation of VERY, / vɛʳʳɪ /?

Do they ever "drop" an R as in a Southern British or Boston pronunciation of CAR, /kɑ /?

Do R and L sound the same in words such as RED and LED, CADILLAC and CATARACT, as in many Asian accents?

Do they pronounce R as /w/ like Marlene Deitrich, /mɑˈwinə ˈditwɪk /?

Do they handle R differently depending on its positioning in a word? Compare the sound of R in:

    –beginning position—RED, RAFT, ROSE
    –middle position—MERRY, AROUND, VIRILE
    –before a vowel in a consonant cluster—CRAFT, TRENCH, STRONG
    –after vowels and before consonants—ART, SEARCH, WORK
    –in final position, after a vowel—CAR, HIRE, HER
    –do they reduce / ɚ / to / ə / as in MOTHER / mʌðə / and EAR / iə /?

Do they use British or American pronunciations of words like BEEN, AGAIN, CLERK, SECRETARY, ISSUE, SCHEDULE, and NECESSARY?

Do they say W words such as WE with / v / as in a German accent / vi /?

Do they say WH words such as WHICH with / w / alone, / wɪtʃ / or with / hw /, / hwɪtʃ / or with / v /, / vɪtʃ /?

Do they say CH in words such as CHERRY with / ʃ / as in a French accent / 'ʃɛˈɪ /?

Do they change / ŋ / to / n / , in words like SONG, / sɔn / or PLAYING /'pleɪɪn /?

Do they change / ŋ / to / ŋg / SONG, / sɔŋg / PLAYING / pleɪɪŋg /?

Do they change / ŋ / to / ŋk / SONG, / sɔŋk / PLAYING / pleɪɪŋk /?

Does / ð / sound like / d / or / z / in words such as THE and ALTHOUGH?

Does / θ / sound like /t / or / s / in words like THINK and ANYTHING?

Do they differentiate voiced and voiceless consonant in the words paired below?

BE	/ bi /	PEA	/ pi /
GAP	/ gæp/	CAP	/ kæp /
DO	/ du /	TO	/ tu /
VAT	/ væt /	FAT	/ fæt /
AZURE	/ 'æʒɚ /	ASHER	/ 'æʃɚ /
HIS	/ hɪz /	HISS	/ hɪs /
EITHER	/ 'iðɚ /	ETHER	/ 'iθɚ /

Do they add "intrusive" sounds such as an R to the word IDEA /aɪˈdiɚ /? Or do they add a weak vowel between two words such as THAT'S NICE /'ðæts əˈnaɪs /?

Do they pronounce the Y in words such as YES as / jes / or / ʤes /? Do they pronounce the J in words such as JOKE as / ʤoʊk / or / joʊk / ?

How do they say the plural S in words that end with a voiced consonant, such as BANDS? Do they pronounce the S as / z / as most native English speakers do / bændz /? Do they pronounce the S as / s /, / bænds /?

How do they pronounce the plural S in words that end in a voiceless consonant, such as HATS? Do they pronounce the S as / s / as most native English speakers do / hæts /? Do they pronounce the S as / z /, / hætz /?

How do they say the plural S in two-syllable words such as BRIDGES, SKETCHES, GLASSES, PHASES? Do they pronounce these as native English speakers do /'brɪʤɪz/? Do they pronounce the S in the second syllable as /s /, /'brɪʤɪs/? Do they try to attach the S to the previous syllable /'brɪʤz/?

How do they pronounce the ED suffix in verbs that end in a voiced consonant, such as RAINED? Do they pronounce the word as one syllable, with a voiced final D / reɪnd /? Do they pronounce the word as one syllable, but with a devoiced final D / reɪnd̥ / or / reɪnt /? Do they add a syllable / ˈreɪnɪd /?

How do they pronounce the ED suffix in verbs ending in a voiceless consonant, such as POPPED? Do they pronounce the word as one syllable with a voiceless final sound / t /, / pɑpt /? Do they pronounce the word as one syllable, but with voiced final sound / d /, / pɑpd /? Do they add a syllable / ˈpɑpɪd /?

How do they pronounce the ED suffix in verbs ending in D and T, such as TRADED and SKATED? Do they pronounce the second syllable, voicing the final D / ˈtreɪdɪd /? Do they pronounce the second syllable, devoicing the final D / ˈtreɪdɪd̥ / or / ˈtreɪdɪt /? Do they attempt to pronounce it as a one-syllable word / ˈtreɪd̩də /?

How do they pronounce the ED in verbs ending with a vowel, such as PLAYED? Do they pronounce the word as one syllable, voicing the final D, / pleɪd /? Do they pronounce the word as one syllable, devoicing the final D, / pleɪd̥ / or / pleɪt /? Do they pronounce the word as two syllables / ˈpleɪɪd /?

Can you hear traces of their native language in the way that they say the following?

The days of the week

The months of the year

The cardinal numbers—one, two, three, etc.

The ordinal numbers—first, second, third, etc.

The letters of the alphabet

The names of cities, states and countries

Do they ever pronounce N as / nj / in words such as NEVER / njɛvɚ / and spinach / ˈspɪnjɪtʃ /?

Do they ever pronounce C as / tʃ / in words such as CINDER / ˈtʃɪndɚ /?

Do they ever pronounce X as / x / in words such as BOX? / x / is the symbol for the voiceless CH sound in the name RACHMANINOFF, or the Gaelic word LOCH.

Do they pronounce / n /, / m / and / l / as complete syllables in words such as OVEN, SPASM and TABLE / ˈʌvn̩ /, / ˈspæzm̩ /, / ˈteɪbl̩ /? Or do they add a vowel / ʌvən /, / ˈspæzəm /, / teɪbəl /?

Is V ever pronounced like / b /? Is the word VOICE pronounced as / bɔɪs /?

Is S pronounced like / z / or / s / in words such as IS and SO?

Is C ever confused with / k / in a word like RECEIVE / riˈkiv /?

Is C ever confused with / s / in a word such as CONCAVE / kɑnˈseɪv /?

Is D formed on the gum ridge, as with most English speakers, in words like DO and ODD? Or is D formed behind the top front teeth, giving it a "thicker," "dental" sound / d̪u /?

Is T formed on the gum ridge in words like TOO, BETTER, and FLAT? Or is T formed behind the top front teeth, giving it a "dental" sound / t̪u /?

Is T ever pronounced as a "glottal stop" / ʔ / in words such as SIT / sɪʔ / or BETTER, / bɛʔɚ /? (/ ʔ / is the symbol for a "glottal stop.")

Is / g / formed further back toward the throat, giving it a guttural sound?

Is / k / formed further back toward the throat, giving it a guttural sound?

Is / h / guttural, causing the sound of friction in the throat / x / in words such as HI / xaɪ /?

Is H dropped in words such as HELLO / ɛˈloʊ / and HAPPEN / ˈæpn̩ / as in a Cockney accent?

Is TH ever pronounced as / f / in words such as THINK and ANYTHING as in a Cockney accent?

Is the TION suffix in a word like CONVERSATION pronounced as / sjɔ̃ / , / ˈkɔ̃veˈsesjɔ̃ / as in a French accent? Is the TION suffix in CONVERSATION pronounced as / tiən /, / kɑnvəˈseɪtiən /?

Is / h / ever added in words such as HONOR / ˈhɑnɚ /?

Is / l / released through the sides of the mouth, giving it a "lateral" sound? Or is it formed with pressure in the back of the tongue, giving it a guttural sound?

Are / n / and / m / ever confused, as in the words TINE and TIME?

Are P, M, or B ever made between the top teeth and the bottom lip, / p̪/, /m̪/ and / b̪/?

Is QU ever pronounced like / k / as in the French pronunciation of QUESTION / kɛstˈjɔ /?

Positioning—Vowels

The words below are grouped, where possible, by vowel sounds occurring in Beginning, Medial and Final positions. Does the pronunciation of the vowel change depending on the position?

/i /   EASE, FEEL, SEE

/ ɪ /   IS, PIN, CITY

/eɪ /   ACHE, PAIN, STAY

/ɛ /   EDGE, SEND

/æ /   AT, SAND

/ a /   ASK, PATH, LAST, STAFF

/ɑ /   FATHER, CALM, AH, SPA

/ɚ /   BETTER, INTERRUPT

/ ɝ /   BIRD, GIRL, HER, STIR

/ ʌ /   UP, STUFF, UH-HUH

/ ə /   ABOUT, PERSONAL, PASTA

/ ɒ / ODD, GOT, WHAT

/ ɔ / ALL, PAWN, STRAW

/oʊ / OWN, STOVE, GO

/ ʊ / HOOD, SHOOK

/ u / OOZE, MOON, TOO

/ aɪ / AISLE, TIME, SHY

/ ɔɪ / OIL, COIN, ANNOY

/ aʊ / OUT, MOUSE, ENDOW

/ ɪɚ / EAR

/ɛɚ / AIR

/ ɑɚ / ARE

/ ɔɚ / OAR

/ ʊɚ / POOR

/ juɚ / CURE

/ɑʊɚ / POWER

/ ɔɪɚ / LAWYER

Vowel Spellings

How does the speaker sound out these words? English spellings can be confusing to people for whom English is a second language. Sometimes sounding out words literally results in a heavier accent. What clues can you discover about someone's accent from the way they read these words? Does pronunciation differ from that of conversation when reading aloud?

/i / HE, BEE, POLICE, WHEAT, KEY, RECEIVE, SHIELD, PEOPLE, MARQUIS

/ ɪ / HIT, GUILD, BEEN, FLYNN, WOMEN, SERVICE, CAPTAIN

/ ɛ / BED, DEAF, SAID, LEONARD, ANY, QUEST

/ æ / THAT, PLAID, GUARANTEE

/ a / CLASS, BATH, CAN'T, ANSWER, ASK, EXAMPLE, RATHER, HALF

/ ɑ / FATHER, CALM, PASTA, SPA, DRAMA

/ ə / ABOUT, A, THE, UPON

/ ʌ / BUT, DOES, BLOOD, TOUCH

/ u / WHO, BOO, CHEW, TRUE, RUE, THROUGH, TWO, SHOE

/ ju / DUE, TUESDAY, STUPID, SUIT, LUNAR, NEW, CUTE, BEAUTY, SKEW, FUEL, HUGE, VIEW

/ ʊ / LOOK, SHOULD, FULL

/ ɔ / SAW, CAUSE, WALK, HALL, BOUGHT, BORE

/ ɒ / WASH, HOT

/ eɪ / FATE, CHAIN, SAY, EIGHT, GAUGE, GREAT

/ aɪ / HI, RYE, SIGH, KITE, SIGN, INDICT, HEIGHT

/ ɔɪ / FOIL, JOY

/ oʊ / GO, BOWL, SEW, COAL, HOLE, COACH, BROOCH, BEAU

/ aʊ / OUT, HOW

Consonant Spellings

How does the speaker sound out these words?

/ t / DOUBT, INDICT, ASKED

/ k / QUACK, AXIS, STOMACH, KARL, CARL

/ gz / EXACT

/ tʃ / MATURE, ITCH, CHASE, CELLO

/ dʒ / JUDGE, GINGER, JAR, IMAGINE

/ m / WOMB, DAMN, CALM

/ n / KNOW, SIGN, GNAW

/ ŋ /   SINK, FINGER, SINGER, TONGUE, BRING

/ f /   LAUGH, PHONE, HALF

/ v /   VOW, STEPHEN, OF

/ ð /—/ θ /   THIS—THIN, EITHER—ETHER, BATHE—BATH

/ s /   PSYCHE, CENTER, ACCENT, RICE, BOX

/ z /   XAVIER, VISOR, IS, EXAMPLE

/ ʃ /   SUGAR, SHUT, ASSURE, PRECIOUS, ACTION

/ ʒ /   MEASURE, REGIME, AZURE, ASIA

/ h /   WHO, WHOSE

/ hw /   WHAT, WHY, WHERE, WHICH, WHITE, WHETHER

/ j /   YOU, IDIOM, USUAL

R Diphthong Spellings

How does the speaker sound out these words?

/ ɪɚ /   FEAR, PEER, TIER, MERE, WEIRD

/ ɛɚ /   AIR, THERE, SCARE, CARE

/ ʊɚ /   DOUR, SURE, BOOR

/ ɔɚ /   BORE, FLOOR, OAR, O'ER

/ ɑɚ /   BAR, ARE, HEARTH, GUARD

/ aɪɚ /   TIRE, BRIAR, PYRE, LIAR

/ aʊɚ /   OUR, TOWER

Positioning—Consonants

A consonant may be pronounced differently, depending on its positioning in a word. It may be pronounced differently initially, medially, and finally. It may change when blended with other consonants or when joined with different vowels. What can you discover about someone's accent by the way he/she reads the following words?

Consonant Combinations:

/b /	/rb/	ORBIT
	/mb/	JUMBO
	/br /	BROWN
	/bl/	BLACK
	/bḷ /	TABLE
	/lb/	ELBOW
	/bs/	ABSENT
	/bz/	JOBS
	beginning	BE
	medial	ABOUT
	final	EBB
/k /	/kt/	FACT
	/kl/	CLASS
	/kḷ /	BUCKLE
	/ks/	BACKSLIDE
	/lk/	ELK
	/rk/	BARK
	/kr/	CROWN
	/sk/	ASK
	/kw/	QUICK
	/skw/	SQUARE
	beginning	KEY
	medial	ACORN
	final	PACK
/d /	/dr/	DRAW
	/rd/	BOARD
	/gd/	OGDEN
	/dʒd/	EDGED
	/ld/	BUILD
	/md/	CAMDEN
	/ðd /	BATHED
	/dv/	ARDVAARK
	beginning	DEAL
	medial	ODOR
	final	ODD
/t /	/tr/	TREND
	/st/	STATE

	/str/	STRAIGHT
	/kt/	ACT
	/tʃt/	ITCHED
	/tw/	TWELVE
	/ts/	HITS
	beginning	TIE
	medial	KITTEN
	final	ATE
/f/	/ft/	SIFT
	/fs/	COUGHS
	/fļ /	AWFUL
	/fl/	FLOOD
	/lf/	ELF
	beginning	FEEL
	medial	OFFEND
	final	IF
/g/	/gw/	UNGUENT
	/gr/	GRAY
	/gļ /	OGLE
	/gl/	GLOW
	/rg/	ARGUE
	/lg/	OLGA
	beginning	GET
	medial	AGO
	final	DOG
/l /	/kl /	CLEANSE
	/kļ /	PICKLE
	/fl /	FLIGHT
	/fl /	RAFFLE
	/gl /	GLEAM
	/ gļ /	STRUGGLE
	/lm /	ELM
	/ mļ /	CAMEL
	/nl /	PANEL
	/lṗ /	HELP
	/pl /	PURPLE
	/lġ /	ILL-GOTTEN
	/ lf /	NAILFILE

	beginning	LET
	medial	ALIVE
	final	OIL

/m/	/mb/	EMBARASS
	/mp/	LAMP
	/mpl̩/	EXAMPLE
	/md/	ROAMED
	/ml̩/	CAMEL
	/rm/	ARM
	/ms/	HIMSELF
	/mz/	JAMS
	/zm̩/	SPASM
	/pm/	UPMAN

	beginning	MOON
	medial	WOMAN
	final	TIME

/n/	/kn/	ACKNOWLEDGE
	/nf/	UNFOLD
	/nd/	LAND
	/nt/	CAN'T
	/ntʃ/	BENCH
	/ndʒ/	CHANGE
	/nl̩/	FINAL
	/ns̩/	TENSE
	/nz/	PENS
	/nθ/	TENTH

	beginning	NO
	medial	ANNOY
	final	PHONE

/p/	/pl/	PLAY
	/pl̩/	PURPLE
	/ps̩/	EPSOM
	/rp/	WARP
	/lp/	HELP
	/mp/	IMPLY

	beginning	PIN
	medial	APPEAR
	final	MAP

/r /	/rθ/	EARTH
	/kr/	CROSS
	/rt/	START
	/rs/	COURSE
	/rz/	CARS
	/tr/	TRAY
	/rb/	HERB
	/br/	BROUGHT
	/pr/	APPRAISE
	/rp/	AIRPORT
	/rk/	PARK
	/gr/	AGREE
	/rg/	ARGUE
	/rʤ/	URGE
	/rtʃ/	PERCH
	beginning	RAIN
	medial	AROUND
	final	ARE
/ʤ /	/rʤ /	BARGE
	/ʤl /	AGILE
	/lʤ /	BULGE
	/ʤɪz /	JUDGES
	beginning	JET
	medial	AGENT
	final	BADGE
/s /	/st/	STAY
	/ts/	SITS
	/ps/	POPS
	/fs/	LAUGHS
	/sk/	SKILL
	/skw/	SQUIRE
	/fs/	COUGHS
	beginning	SEE
	medial	ESSAY
	final	TOSS
/ʃ/	/rʃ/	HARSH
	/ʃr/	SHRINK
	/ʃt/	PUSHED
	/kʃ/	ACTION

	/ʃl̩ /	BUSHEL
	/ʃn̩ /	OCEAN
	/ʃɪz/	WASHES
	beginning	SHE
	medial	ASSURE
	final	FLASH
/θ/	/rθ/	EARTH
	/θr/	THROW
	/fθ/	FIFTH
	/fθs/	FIFTHS
	/θl̩ /	ETHYL
	/nθ/	TENTH
	beginning	THIN
	medial	ETHER
	final	PATH
/ð/	/ðd/	BATHED
	/ðz/	LATHES
	beginning	THEN
	medial	EITHER
	final	WRITHE
/v/	/rv/	SERVE
	/lv/	TWELVE
	/lvz/	ELVES
	/vd/	LOVED
	/vz/	LOAVES
	/vl̩ /	OVAL
	/vn̩ /	OVEN
	beginning	VERB
	medial	EVER
	final	SLEEVE
/w/	/kw/	QUART
	/dw/	DWINDLE
	/tw/	TWITCH
	/gw/	GWEN
	/rw/	ORWELL
	/sw/	SWELL
	/ʃw/	SCHWINN

		beginning	WIN
		medial	AWAY
/hw /	/rhw/	OVERWHELM
	/rst hw/	ERSTWHILE
		beginning	WHICH
		medial	AWHILE
/z /	/bz/	CABS
	/dz/	TRADES
	/gz/	BAGS
	/nz/	BEGINS
	/mz/	EXAMS
	/lz/	SELLS
	/ŋz/	SINGS
	/zd/	AMUSED
	/zl /	PUZZLE
	/zm/	ENTHUSIASM
	/rz/	POURS
	/vz/	LOVES
	/ʤɪz/	AGES
	/tʃɪz/	ITCHES
	/zɪz/	CLOSES
	/sɪz/	GLASSES
		beginning	ZOO
		medial	AZALEA
		final	RAISE
/tʃ/	/rtʃ/	SEARCH
	/tʃt/	PITCHED
	/ltʃ/	BELCH
	/ntʃ/	INCH
	/tʃɪz/	FETCHES
		beginning	CHIN
		medial	MATURE
		final	ETCH
/ʒ /		medial	PLEASURE
		final	MIRAGE
/ŋ/	/ŋg /	FINGER
	/ŋk /	THINK

95

/ŋk ̣l/	ANKLE
medial	SINGER
final	ALONG

| / j / | beginning | YOU |
| | medial | ONION |

The Lilt of an Accent

Every accent approaches language a little differently. The sound of an accent is determined not only by vowel and consonant changes but by the use of PITCH, VOLUME and RHYTHM as well. Together, the elements of PITCH, VOLUME and RHYTHM create the LILT of the accent.

Pitch

Although the human voice is capable of several octaves of range, the speaking range is usually much narrower. For speaking, people tend to settle into one part of the voice—one register. Is your accent donor speaking in their upper, middle, or lower register?

Drift

Because the voice isn't absolutely fixed in one part of the range, you may hear it drift into a higher or lower register if one speaks for any length of time. Does the voice tend to drift higher during long phrases? Does the voice tend to drift lower during long phrases? Does the voice maintain the same register?

Inflections

What kinds of inflections do you hear in the voice? Do you hear upward inflections? Do you hear downward inflections? Do you hear a monotone throughout an entire phrase? When do inflections tend to happen?

Do you hear upward inflections at the end of phrases?

> you
> how are

Do you hear upward inflections in the middle of phrases?

> are you
> how

Do you hear downward inflections at the end of phrases?

> how are
> you

Do you hear downward inflections in the middle of phrases?

> how
>   are   you

Does pitch ever "bend" up or down within a single word? Does the pitch of a word bend upward?

>   u
>   o
>   how are y

Does the pitch of a word bend downward?
>   how a
>   re you

Intervals

Are phrases spoken in monotone, or do you hear shifts in pitch from word to word? Are the intervals large and obvious?

>   are
>
>   how   you

Are the intervals small and subtle?

>   are
>   how   you

Do you hear intervals of a semitone at a time? Do you hear intervals that are one full tone or wider? Are intervals used to emphasize words?

>   see
>   it's nice to   you

Is the transition from one pitch to another gradual? Is the transition from one pitch to another abrupt? Is there a glissando flow from pitch to pitch within a phrase?

>   u
>   o
>   y
>   e
>   r
>   a
>   w
>   o
>   h

Are intervals sudden with spiky sounding transitions?

                         are
              how
                              you

Rhythm

How do the sounds flow within a word? Are vowel sounds elongated into a drawl?

kʊ::d	ju::	hæ::v	noʊ::n	haʊ::	oʊ::ld	ðə::	toʊ::st	ɪ::z
Could	you	have	known	how	old	the	toast	is?

A double colon, / :: / or a triple colon / ::: / indicates double or triple elongation. The colon, widely used as a marking to elongate vowels, is used below to modify consonants as well. In the case of continuant consonants, the colon indicates elongation. In the case of all other consonants, the colon indicates greater muscularity or intensity in the formation of sound.

Are vowels clipped short by energetic, muscular consonants?

kʊd:	ju	hæv:	non:	haʊ	old:	ðə	tost:	ɪz:
Could	you	have	known	how	old	the	toast	is?

In general, are consonants precisely and meticulously formed? Or are they loosely and sloppily formed?

Are stop consonants / b /, / p /, / d /, / t /, / g /, and / k / ever held for a pause before they are released? The p... (Hold the formation of the P for a beat before releasing it)...pen   / ðəp‚pɛn /. I'll g...get it / aɪl g‚gɛt ɪt /. We d...don't know / wi d‚doʊnt noʊ /

Are double consonants held and released, as in the Italian language?

HAPPY	/ ˈhæp‚pɪ /	DIMMER	/ ˈdɪm‚mɚ /
LADDER	/ ˈlæd‚dɚ /	SUNNY	/ ˈsʌn‚nɪ /
SHUFFLE	/ ˈʃʌf‚fl̩ /	PEPPER	/ ˈpɛp‚pɚ /
BAGGY	/ ˈbæg‚gɪ /	LETTUCE	/ ˈlɛt‚tɪs /

Is the rate of the words (i.e. syllables per minute) fast, medium, or slow?

Do you ever hear the rate accelerate?
    h o w   a r e y o u today

Do you ever hear the rate decelerate?
    howare y o u   t o d a   y

How long are the silences (pauses) between words? Are pauses rare or common? Do pauses last 1/2 a beat? One beat? Two beats? Three beats? Are pauses used for emphasis—framing thoughts?

I don't (one beat pause) think so.

Is the rhythm even—are most syllables of the same length? Is the rhythm unpredictable—are syllables of markedly different lengths?

How ARE you toDAY / haʊ ˈɑːɚ ju təˈdeɪː /

Is the rhythm smooth and legato? Or is the rhythm a jabbing staccato? Staccato rhythm can be the result of a glottal stop preceding each word / ʔ /. The transcription of the following sentence indicates a glottally-induced stacatto rhythm:

How   are   you / haʊʔɑɚˈʔju /

How is rhythm used for stress and emphasis?

Volume

Is the volume loud, soft, or in between? When does volume shift? Does volume increase in the middle of a phrase?

how ARE you

Does the volume decrease in the middle of a phrase?

HOW are YOU

Does the volume increase at the end of a phrase?

how are YOU

Does the volume decrease at the end of a phrase?

HOW ARE you

Do phrases crescendo?

ʜᴏWAREYOU

Do phrases decrescendo?

HOWAREʏᴏᴜ

Pronunciation Game

Work with one accent at a time. Use the key-word transcriptions for someone else's accent from your accent chart, and the phonetic pillows to infuse your body with new pronunciations.

Pick a word from your accent chart that contrasts with the way you speak. Say the word in your accent and in the contrasting accent. Now grab the pillow that has this contrasting sound.

Use the pillow to move the sound through your body, until the sound is well established. Now say the whole word in this unfamiliar way, continuing to let the pillow enliven the sound in your body.

As you explore this sound and word, let it move you through the space, so that you randomly encounter other people and their sounds. With each person, use your sound/word in dialogue with their sound/word. Continue this exchange for as long as you like, then throw the pillow away and say the word as simply as you can.

Continue through the rest of the word contrasts for this accent in the same way.

French Accent: Strong Vowel Changes

SCENE / ɪ /
/ ɪ / changes to / i /

HIP / hɪp /		/ ip /
GLIB / glɪb /		/ glib /
BEING / ˈbiɪŋ /		/ bi iŋ /

"I'm HIP to the GLIB gab BEING by the MILL but WILL the CHIN CONVINCE?"

SCENE / eɪ /
/ eɪ / changes to / e /

THEY / ðeɪ /		/ ze /
SAKE / seɪk /		/ sek /
RAGE / reɪdʒ /		/ ˈeʒ /

"Who do THEY think THEY are?
I did it for my mother's SAKE and
the RAGE is building in my heart."

SCENE / oʊ /
/ oʊ / changes to / o /

KNOWN / noʊn /   / non /
TOAST / toʊst /   / tost /
OLD / oʊld /   / old /

"Could you have KNOWN how OLD the TOAST is?"

SCENE / ʊ /
/ ʊ / changes to / u /

COOK / kʊk /   / kuk /
SUGAR / ʃʊgɚ /   / ʃugeʳ /
GOOD / gʊd /   / gud /

"Where's my GOOD COOK
hiding her SUGAR supplies?"

SCENE / u /
/ u / changes to / y̶ /

TRUE / tru /   / tʳy̶ /
YOU'VE / juv /   / jy̶v /
CLUE / klu /   / kly̶ /

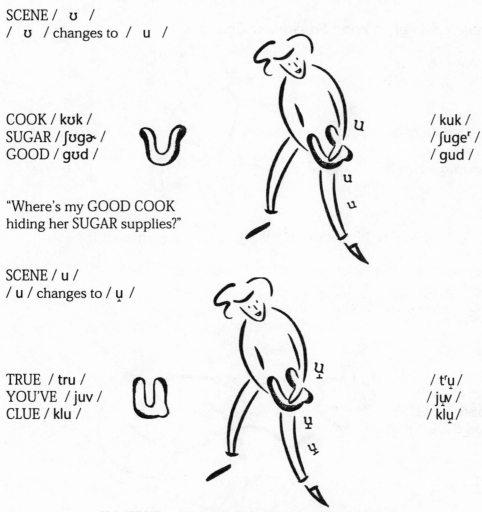

"It's TRUE then that YOU'VE been watching CLUE
after CLUE come bristling THROUGH?"

SCENE / ɔ /
/ ɔ / changes to / o /

BOUGHT / bɔt /   / bot /
WALL / wɔl /   / wol /
AUCTION / 'ɔkʃn̩ /   / 'okʃen /

"They BOUGHT the bit of WALL at the AUCTION."

French Accent: Strong Consonant Changes

SCENE / h /
/ h / is silent / ȟ/

/ 'hʌvɚ / HOVER   / 'ʌveʳ /
/ hɪɚ / HERE   / ieʳ /
/ hoʊpɪŋ / HOPING   / op'iŋ /

"I HOVER HERE and there HOPING to keep them from HIDING."

SCENE / ʤ /
/ ʤ / changes to / ʒ /

/ ɛʤ / EDGE   / eʒ /
/ bæʤ / BADGE   / bæʒ /
/ lɒʤd / LODGED   / lʌʒd /

"It's at the EDGE of my BADGE but it seems LODGED on the sharp star EDGE."

SCENE / r /
  / r / becomes / ʳ /

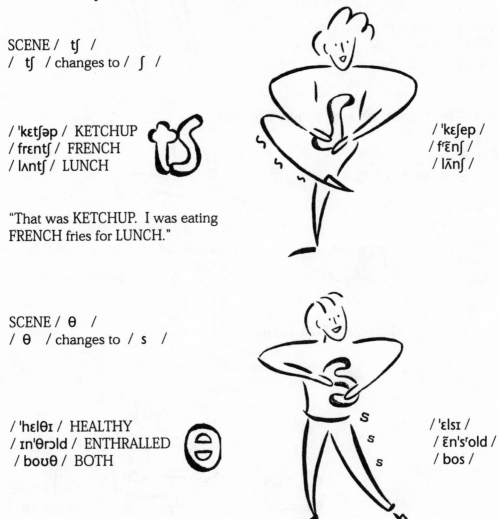

/ ˈpɛrɪʃ / PERISH	/ pɜ'ʳiʃ /
/ ˈtærɪ / TARRY	/ tæ'ʳi /
/ frɒm / FROM	/ fʳʌm /

"It may PERISH if we TARRY FROM its CORNER of the CELLAR."

SCENE / tʃ /
  / tʃ / changes to / ʃ /

/ ˈkɛtʃəp / KETCHUP	/ ˈkɛʃep /
/ frɛntʃ / FRENCH	/ fʳɛ̃ʃ /
/ lʌntʃ / LUNCH	/ lãʃ /

"That was KETCHUP. I was eating
FRENCH fries for LUNCH."

SCENE / θ /
  / θ / changes to / s /

/ ˈhɛlθɪ / HEALTHY	/ ˈɛlsɪ /
/ ɪnˈθrɔld / ENTHRALLED	/ ɛ̃n'sʳold /
/ boʊθ / BOTH	/ bos /

"HEALTHY, she is ENTHRALLED BOTH by our
wedding and her approaching day."

SCENE / ð /
/ ð / changes to / z /

/ beɪð / BATHE / bez /
/ ðɛn / THEN / zen /
/suð d/ SOOTHED / su̱zd /

"BATHE yourself in ideas, THEN come
to THE setting to have your sweating
brow SOOTHED."

German Accent: Strong Vowel Changes

SCENE / eɪ /
/ eɪ / changes to / e: /

/ geɪn / GAIN / ge:n /
/ pleɪ / PLAY / ple: /
/ feɪd / FADE / fe:d̪ /

"It could be our GAIN if the PLAY FADES."

SCENE / æ /
/ æ / changes to / ɛ /

/ ræŋ / RANG / ˈɛŋ /
/ læd / LAD / lɛd /
/ læŋgwɪdʒ / LANGUAGE /ˈlɛŋgvɪd̪ʒ /

"I RANG the LAD AND he used
LANGUAGE AS though it were AN AX."

SCENE / a /
/ a / changes to / ɑ /

/ raðɚ / RATHER
/ bask / BASK
/ paθ / PATH

/ ˈɑðɚ̥ /
/ b̥ɑsk /
/ pɑs /

"I'd RATHER BASK in the PATH
of my MASTER than fight a RAFT
of NASTY bowls of chowder."

SCENE / oʊ /
/ oʊ / changes to / o /

/ noʊ / KNOW
/ loʊd / LOAD
/ oʊts / OATS

/ no /
/ lod̥ /
/ ots /

"I KNOW you want a LOAD of OATS to make that
GROTESQUE OKRA pound cake."

SCENE / ʌ /
/ ʌ / becomes / a /

/ mʌg / MUG
/ mʌd / MUD
/ lʌv / LOVE

/ mag /
/ mad̥ /
/ lav̥ /

"A MUG of MUD pie LOVE JUST for you."

SCENE / ə /
/ ə / changes to / a /

/ əˈgri /   AGREE
/ əˈkaʊnt /   ACCOUNT
/ əˈtæk /   ATTACK

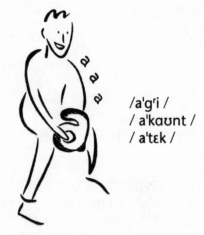

/aˈgʳi /
/ aˈkaʊnt /
/ aˈtɛk /

"I do not AGREE with the ACCOUNT of the ATTACK."

German Accent: Strong Consonant Changes

SCENE / b /
/ b / becomes / b̥ /

/ tjubz /   TUBES
/ bɜbn /   BOURBON
/ bɒks̩ /   BOX

/ tub̥z /
/b̥ɜʳbn /
/ b̥ɒks /

"TUBES of BOURBON then,
in a BOX of BLEACHED corn."

SCENE / d /
/ d / becomes / d̥ /

/ ˈidɪkt /   EDICT
/ekˈspouzd/   EXPOSED
/ blaɪnd /   BLIND

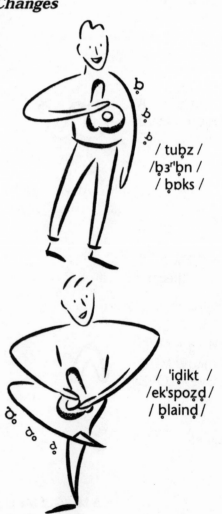

/ ˈid̥ɪkt /
/ekˈspozd̥ /
/ blaind̥ /

"The EDICT EXPOSED
our collaborations, but
was BLIND to our own
BIRD in the HAND."

SCENE / g /
/ g / changes to / g̊ /

/ peɪŋgwɪn / PENGUIN
/ graʊl / GROWL
/ 'gɔkɪŋ / GAWKING

/ peŋ'gvɪn /
/ g̊raʊl /
/ 'gɔkɪŋk̊ /

"The PENGUIN upstarts GROWL
about GAWKING at GOD."

SCENE / dʒ /
/ dʒ / changes to / d̥ʒ /

/ dʒɛt / JET
/ eɪdʒd / AGED
/ 'dʒusɪz / JUICES

/ d̥ʒɛt /
/ ed̥ʒd /
/ 'd̥ʒusɪz̥ /

"JET black GERBIL AGED in the JUICES of a hamster."

SCENE / ŋ /
/ ŋ / becomes / ŋk /

/ 'bæŋɪŋ / BANGING
/ gɒŋ / GONG
/ sɪŋ / SING

/ 'b̥eŋɪŋk /
/ gɒŋk /
/ s̊ɪŋk /

"Stop BANGING the GONG...then SING to me."

107

SCENE / r /
/ r / becomes / ʳ /

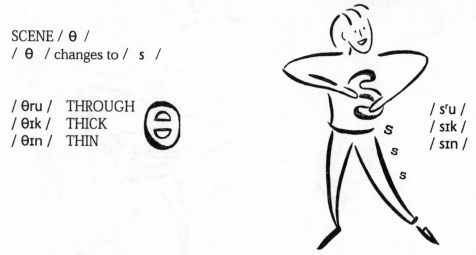

/ ˈbɔɚɪŋ / BORING   / ˈbɔˈɪŋk /
/ ˈkɔɚəs / CHORUS   / ˈkɔˈəs /
/ ˈdrɪŋkɪŋ / DRINKING / ˈdˈɪŋkɪŋk /

"The BORING CHORUS of chablis DRINKING CONQUERORS."

SCENE / θ /
/ θ / changes to / s /

/ θru / THROUGH   / sʳu /
/ θɪk / THICK   / sɪk /
/ θɪn / THIN   / sɪn /

"THROUGH THICK and THIN, our EARTH warrants we come upon a HEARTH."

SCENE / ð /
/ ð / changes to / d /

/ ɔlˈðoʊ / ALTHOUGH   / olˈdo /
/ ðə / THE   / də /
/ ˈsmʌðɚɪŋ / SMOTHERING   / ˈsmadəˈɪŋk /

"ALTHOUGH we feel THE two are SMOTHERING one ANOTHER."

SCENE / w /
/ w / becomes / v /

/ dwɛl / DWELL
/ twɛlv / TWELVE
/ swɪs / SWISS

/ dvɛl /
/ tvɛlv̥ /
/ svɪs /

"DWELL on this. The TWELVE
SWISS tenors WORE dwarf suits
that twinned them."

SCENE / hw /
/ hw / changes to / v /

/ ˈhwɪmpɚ / WHIMPER
/ hwaɪt / WHITE
/ ˈhwɪskɪ / WHISKEY

/ ˈvɪmpɚ /
/ vaɪt /
/ ˈvɪskɪ /

"WHIMPER WITH me turn WHITE as they pretend to offer WHISKEY."

SCENE / ʒ /
/ ʒ / changes to / ʒ̥ /

/ ˈkæʒuəl / CASUAL
/ ˈvɪʒn / VISION
/ ˈtrɛʒɚ / TREASURE

/ ˈkɛʒ̥uəl /
/ ˈvɪʒ̥n /
/ ˈtʳɛʒ̥ɚ /

"I want this to be a CASUAL affair and a VISION
of great joy...they should TREASURE."

SCENE / v /
/ v / changes to / v̥ /

/ ˈvɪktə˞ɪ / VICTORY   / v̥ɪktə˞ɪ /
/ ɛnˈlaɪvnd / ENLIVENED   / ɛnˈlaɪv̥nd /
/ ˈvɪvɪd / VIVID   / ˈv̥ɪv̥ɪd /

"VICTORY, I feel ENLIVENED
by the VIVID feel of being INVINCIBLE."

SCENE / s /
/ s / becomes / z /

/ gɛs / GUESS   / gez /
/ sɔs / SAUCE   / sɔz /
/ naɪs / NICE   / naɪz /

"I GUESS a little SAUCE might be NICE."

Inventing Language Part Two

(See game #1, page 43)

This is a game to practice the lilt of an accent, using random sounds as "words" and "phrases."

Focus on one accent at a time. Make a pile of all the voiced-sound pillows. Move one pillow after another over your body, releasing its sound. Let the sounds flow together as if they were words and let these "words" flow together into "phrases". The result will be somewhat like speaking gibberish, except that the sounds are dictated by the pillows you encounter rather than by your own whim. Use these words and phrases to practice the lilt changes needed for the accent. Ask yourself the following questions, and incorporate the lilt patterns you explored on pages (96-99) into your gibberish words and phrases.

Begin with the pitch changes needed in the accent:

How often does pitch change?

Do pitch changes ever happen within a single word?

Where do pitch changes tend to occur within a phrase?
Does pitch ever change at the beginning of a new phrase?
Does pitch ever change in the middle of a phrase?
Does pitch ever change at the end of a phrase?
Are pitch intervals between sounds large or small?
Are they semitones?
Are they several notes?
How wide is the range of your voice in this accent?
Is your range only a few notes?
Is your range an octave or more?

After you've gotten a feeling for the pitch changes of the accent, continue creating words and phrases as above but focus on the volume patterns of the accent rather than the pitch. For this part of the game, use all the phonetic pillows, both voiced and voiceless.

When does the volume change?
When does volume increase?
When does volume decrease?
Does volume change occur in the beginning of a new phrase?
Does it change in the middle of a phrase?
Does it change at the end of a phrase?
Does volume ever change within a single word?
Does volume change abruptly?
Does volume change gradually?
Does volume crescendo?
Does volume decrescendo?
Does volume pulse rhythmically back and forth from loud to soft?
Do you stay on your voice in this accent?
Does your voice become guttaral or breathy in this accent?

Continue the game as above, but now focus on the length of sounds.

Are certain sounds elongated in this accent?
Are certain sounds shortened in this accent?
Are sounds longer in the beginning of phrases?
Are sounds longer in the middle of phrases? In the end of phrases?
Are words drawled?
Are words clipped?

Now focus on the rhythms of the accent.

Is the overall tempo of the accent fast or slow?
Does the tempo ever change within a phrase?
Do phrases ever start slow and then speed up?
Do phrases ever start fast and then slow down?
Is the rhythm of the accent legato?
Is the rhythm of the accent staccato?
Are plosive sounds / b /, / p /, / d /, / t /, / g /, and / k / explosive and active?
Are plosive sounds unreleased and passive?

Do certain sounds recede, or disappear?
Do certain sounds get slurred?
Do certain sounds get over-articulated?

"Changing Key": A Game to Learn Accents

Begin playing with the pillows one at a time in random order, moving them around your body and releasing their sounds. After you've gotten through all of the pillows a couple of times (or after a few minutes), switch from saying the sound the way you usually do to the way it changes in an accent. For instance, if you switch to a British accent, the sound / oʊ / will change to /əʊ/. But rather than finding the / əʊ / pillow just "change key." You'll still be playing with / oʊ / but pronouncing it / əʊ /. Continue through the rest of the pillows in this accent and notice that some pillows don't change at all and others may change their "lilt" a little bit without actually changing from one sound to another.

This game requires familiarity with phonetic symbols and the accents being used. It may be helpful to have a key for the pronunciation contrasts handy to refer to if you get stuck. But refer to it only when absolutely necessary so that exploration of the accent remains very physical. With this game you can begin to convince your body that all accents are a part of you. That genuine communication is possible in any accent as long as the sounds of that accent are rooted to the same impulses and desire as your more familiar everyday speaking.

Changing key from / oʊ / to / əʊ /.

Comparison of British, U.S., and "Good Speech for Classic Texts"

The following is a comparison of three accents: "Good Speech for Classic Texts," a second, more colloquial "General American Accent," and a British accent that fits the description of "received pronunciation." Notice the many similarities between "Good Speech for Classic Texts" and "received pronunciation." It has been said that "Good Speech for Classic Texts" was gleaned from the sounds of North America, but whoever did the gleaning chose the North American sounds that came closest to those of southern British speech.

SCENE / ju / (in words like DUKE, SUIT, TUNE)

	British accent	U.S. accent	"Good Speech for Classic Texts"
NUDE	/njud/	/ nud /	/njud/
TUNA	/'tjunə/	/'tunə/	/'tjunə/
TUNE	/ tjun /	/tun/	/tjun/
ASSUME	/ ə'sjum /	/ə'sum/	/ə'sjum/

"The NUDE TUNA is droning on a TUNE I ASSUME you know."

SCENE / ɚ /

	British accent	U.S. accent	"Good Speech for Classic Texts"
DINNER	/ 'dɪnə /	/ 'dɪnɚ /	/ 'dɪnə /
GLIMMER	/ 'glɪmə /	/ 'glɪmɚ /	/ 'glɪmə /

"Don't come home for DINNER if there's not a GLIMMER of hope for us."

SCENE / ɪɚ /

	British accent	U.S. accent	"Good Speech for Classic Texts"
HEAR	/ hɪə /	/ hɪɚ /	/ hɪə /
SNEER	/ snɪə /	/ snɪɚ /	/ snɪə /

"I HEAR you've got a contract. Don't SNEER at my contract."

SCENE / ɛɚ /

	British accent	U.S. accent	"Good Speech for Classic Texts"
CHAIR	/ tʃɛə /	/ tʃɛɚ /	/ tʃɛə /
DARE	/ dɛə /	/ dɛɚ /	/ dɛə /
HAIR	/ hɛə /	/ hɛɚ /	/ hɛə /

113

"When the CHAIR is encircled by the spiritual sphere do we
DARE to revolve in our plastered down HAIR?"

SCENE / ɑɚ /

	British accent	U.S. accent	"Good Speech for Classic Texts"
	ɑ:	**ɑɚ**	**ɑ:**
CARBON	/ ˈkɑːbn̩ /	/ ˈkɑɚˑbn̩ /	/ kɑːbn̩ /
BARB	/ bɑːb /	/ bɑɚˑb /	/ bɑːb /
CARD	/ kɑːd /	/ kɑɚˑd /	/ kɑːd /
SHARP	/ ʃɑːp /	/ ʃɑɚˑp /	/ ʃɑːp /

"CARBON tested BARB. The CARD is SHARP."

SCENE / ɔɚ /

	British accent	U.S. accent	"Good Speech for Classic Texts"
	ɔ:	**ɔɚ**	**ɔ:**
PORK	/ pɔːk /	/ pɔɚk /	/ pɔːk /
ORGANS	/ ˈɔːgɪnz /	/ ˈɔɚˑgɪnz /	/ ˈɔːgɪnz /
FOR	/ fɔː /	/ fɔɚ /	/ fɔə /

"PORK ORGANS FOR supper."

SCENE / a / (Don't confuse with /æ / see pronunciation rule on page 34)

	British accent	U.S. accent	"Good Speech for Classic Texts"
	a	**æ**	**a**
RATHER	/ ˈraðə /	/ ˈræðɚ /	/ raðə /
BASK	/ bask /	/ bæsk /	/ bask /
PATH	/ paθ /	/ pæθ /	/ paθ /
PASTOR	/ ˈpastə /	/ ˈpæstɚ /	/ pastə /

"I'd RATHER BASK in the PATH of my PASTOR than fight a
RAFT of NASTY bowls of chowder."

SCENE / oʊ /

British accent	U.S. accent	"Good Speech for Classic Texts"

	British accent	U.S. accent	"Good Speech for Classic Texts"
KNOWN	/ nəʊn /	/ noʊn /	/ noʊn /
OLD	/ əʊld /	/ oʊld /	/ oʊld /
TOAST	/ təʊst /	/ toʊst /	/ toʊst /

"Could you have KNOWN how OLD the TOAST is?"

SCENE / ɝ /

	British accent	U.S. accent	"Good Speech for Classic Texts"
JERK	/ dʒɜːk /	/ dʒɝk /	/ dʒɜːk /
LURKS	/ lɜːks /	/ lɝks /	/ lɜːks /
SEARCH	/ sɜːtʃ /	/ sɝtʃ /	/ sɜːtʃ /

"When that JERK LURKS in SEARCH of his collection of mollusks, I shall STIR his cornflakes."

SCENE / ʊɚ /

	British accent	U.S. accent	"Good Speech for Classic Texts"

POOR	/ pʊə /	/ pʊɚ /	/ pʊə /
ASSURE	/ əˈʃʊə /	/ əˈʃʊɚ /	/ əˈʃʊə /
DOUR	/ dʊə /	/ dʊɚ /	/ dʊə /

"The POOR ASSURE...we cannot be DOUR."

SCENE / aɪɚ /

	British accent	U.S. accent	"Good Speech for Classic Texts"

REQUIRE	/ rɪˈkwaɪə /	/ rɪˈkwaɪɚ /	/ rɪˈkwaɪə /
INQUIRE	/ ɪnˈkwaɪə /	/ ɪnˈkwaɪɚ /	/ ɪnˈkwaɪə /
ADMIRE	/ ædˈmaɪə /	/ ædˈmaɪɚ /	/ ædˈmaɪə /

115

"Don't REQUIRE me to INQUIRE about who you ADMIRE."

SCENE / ɔɪɚ /

	British accent	U.S. accent	"Good Speech for Classic Texts"
	ɔɪə	ɔɪɚ	ɔɪə
SAWYER	/ ˈsɔɪə /	/ ˈsɔɪɚ /	/ ˈsɔɪə /
LAWYER	/ ˈlɔɪə /	/ ˈlɔɪɚ /	/ ˈlɔɪə /

"SAWYER will meet the LAWYER."

SCENE / aʊɚ /

	British accent	U.S. accent	"Good Speech for Classic Texts"
	aʊə	aʊɚ	aʊə
SCOUR	/ ˈskaʊə /	/ ˈskaʊɚ /	/ ˈskaʊə /
SHOWER	/ ˈʃaʊə /	/ ˈʃaʊɚ /	/ ˈʃaʊə /

"I was just about to SCOUR the SHOWER curtain."

SCENE / ɒ /

	British accent	U.S. accent	"Good Speech for Classic Texts"
		ɑ	
COMEDY	/ˈkɒmədɪ /	/ˈkamədɪ/	/ˈkɒmədɪ/
ODD	/ɒd/	/ad/	/ɒd/
SCHOLAR	/ˈskɒlə/	/ˈskalɚ/	/ˈskɒlə/

"WHAT COMEDY this NOD to the POSSIBLE INVOLVEMENT OF GOD is the RELIGION OF the ODD COLLEGE SCHOLAR."

Or in words like WAS, OF, WHAT, and FROM

	ɒ	ʌ	ɒ
WHAT	/hwɒt/	/hwʌt/	/hwɒt/
OF	/ɒv/	/ʌv/	/ɒv/
WAS	/wɒz/	/wʌz/	/wɒz/
FROM	/frɒm/	/frʌm/	/frɒm/

Sound Changes used in "Good Speech for Classic Texts"

The vowel in ASK is pronounced as /a /, / ask /
The vowel in ODD is pronounced as / ɒ /, /ɒd /
The vowel in TUNE is pronounced as / ju / , / tjun /
The ER in JERK is pronounced as /ɜ /, /dʒɜk /

The uses of R in this accent are the same as British (see below.)

Sound Changes used in a British Accent

The vowel in ASK is pronounced as /ɑ /, /ɑsk /
The vowel in ODD is pronounced as /ɒ /, /ɒd /
The vowel in GO is pronounced as /əʊ /, / gəʊ /
The vowel in CALL is pronounced as /ɔ: /, /kɔ:l /
The vowel in TUNE is pronounced as /ju /, /tjun /
The ER in JERK is pronounced as /ɜ /, / dʒɜk /

Different Uses of R in a British Accent

Listen to a British person read the R and R dipthong scenes from the play. Notice whether they ever tap-trill an R. Notice if they ever link a final R onto the next word (see examples below.) Play around with the different types of R; the more you use tap-trills and R linking, the more extreme the accent will be.

R between two vowels within the same word: a) Link the R to the second vowel; b) Tap-trill the R. A tap trill is a single trill of the tip of the tongue against the gum ridge. Think of it as a very soft, small d.

> "BURROW into the HEROIC SURRENDER and WORRY the BORING CHORUS."

R between a vowel and a consonant within the same word: The R is not sounded.

> "We've CONVERTED the TARGET into the ARGOT he knows."

R at the end of a word followed by a word that begins with a consonant: The R is not sounded.

> "That PYRE LIAR was out to GORE, the other means to IN-SPIRE, then retire."

R at the end of a word followed by a word that begins with a vowel: a) Link the R onto the vowel that begins the next word; b) In an extreme accent, tap-trill the R.

> "the OBSCURE emotions...the ALLURE of aftershave"

R at the end of a sentence: The R is not sounded if you come to a full stop. If no pause is taken between this word and the word beginning the next sentence, proceed as above.

When I was three, my family moved from New Jersey to California. We were strangers in a strange land. A girlfriend of my sister's would say, "Let's go to your house and listen to your mother tawk." My accent sharply contrasted that of Californian toddlers: I drew O words into two syllables, such as / 'koʊ ʌld / (cold) and / 'oʊ ʌld / (old). I remember phonics being presented to my class in first grade with the use of a black felt board on which clung a picture of a zebra and a felt letter Z. I believed even then that these felt symbols should be stuffed loosely with dried beans and flung around the room. Instead, we stared at them in wonderment, occasionally sounding out a word. It was sounding out words that got me in trouble. I remember being taken aside with a couple of other students by an older man and doing something he called "speech." We sat on benches in a small, makeshift classroom and repeated words the way he said them, or identified the names of objects in pictures. I remember flashcards, and a little girl who had trouble making her s's. After three sessions or so the man smiled at me and said I wouldn't have to have "speech" anymore. He realized (I like to think) that the phonics lessons had diagnosed in me, not a speech disorder, but merely a New Jersey accent, which he decided to let me keep. He was my first speech teacher, and though he taught me nothing, he had enough class to take nothing away.

A student actor at New York University was so opposed to having his Iowan accent corrected that he bit his speech teacher. As a result of this incident he was suspended. Twenty years later he still acts with an Iowa accent. In New England. In plays by Shakespeare.

> The subtle charm of the genuine pronunciation
> is not in dictionaries, grammars, marks of accent,
> formulas of language, or in any laws or rules.
> The charm of the genuine pronunciation of all words of all tongues,
> is in natural, flexible vocal organs and in a developed harmonious soul.
> All words spoken from these have deeper, simpler sounds, new meanings,
> impossible on any less terms!!!
> —Adapted from Walt Whitman's *American Primer.*

The Sounds in Sonnets

Sounds are not equally represented in language—some occur very frequently, others quite seldom. Most sounds will occur several times in a passage of one hundred words. Studies show that sounds tend to occur at the same rate of frequency in all styles of literature, as well as conversation. / ə /, / ɪ /, / n /, / t /, / r /, / d / and / s / are some of the most common sounds; each may occur seven or more times per hundred words. On the other hand, / θ / and / ju / each occur about every one hundred twenty-five words; / ɔɪ / every three hundred fifty words; and / ʒ / every one thousand words.

Shakespeare's sonnets, because they are about one hundred words each, give your mouth a chance to experience almost all the sounds of English at least once in their fourteen lines. The sonnets have a good sound distribution, and many of them contain all of the sounds that you've worked with in this book (with the exception of the very rare / ʒ /—though a few of the sonnets even contain that sound.) The point here is not that the best sonnets are those that use the greatest variety of sounds, but rather that in order to relate something universal, you may end up using every possible sound to get the job done.

In the sonnet below, the first appearance of each vowel sound is noted with a phonetic symbol. This is to illustrate that every vowel sound appears in the sonnet at least once.

Sonnet 65

    ɪ   a (æ)   ɔ   oʊ   ɝ   aʊ   i
SINCE BRASS, NOR STONE, NOR EARTH, NOR BOUNDLESS SEA,

   ʌ   æ   eɪ   ɚ
BUT SAD MORTALITY O'ERSWAYS THEIR POWER,

                   ju   ə
HOW WITH THIS RAGE SHALL BEAUTY HOLD A PLEA,

  u
WHOSE ACTION IS NO STRONGER THAN A FLOWER?

                   ɛ
O, HOW SHALL SUMMER'S HONEY BREATH HOLD OUT

AGAINST THE WRACKFUL SIEGE OF BATTERING DAYS,

    ɒ(ɑ)   ɑ
WHEN ROCKS IMPREGNABLE ARE NOT SO STOUT,

               aɪ
NOR GATES OF STEELE SO STRONG BUT TIME DECAYS?

O, FEARFUL MEDITATION, WHERE, ALACK,

SHALL TIME'S BEST JEWEL FROM TIME'S CHEST LIE HID?

                        ʊ
OR WHAT STRONG HAND CAN HOLD HIS SWIFT FOOT BACK,

   ɔɪ
OR WHO HIS SPOIL OF BEAUTY CAN FORBID?

O, NONE, UNLESS THIS MIRACLE HATH MIGHT,

THAT IN BLACK INK MY LOVE MAY STILL SHINE BRIGHT.

Speak this sonnet a few times. Be aware of its wide variety of sounds. Does it ask a lot of your mouth? Notice whether you're saying the vowels in the same way that I've written them down. Probably sometimes you are and sometimes you are not. We don't all form our vowels in exactly the same way, and we don't all use the same vowel in the pronunciation of the same word. Go back through the sonnet now and rewrite any of the sounds the way you say them. Now see how many consonants you can find in the sonnet, and mark them in the text. I found that every consonant (except the rare / ʒ / was there at least once. But don't take my word for it. Find them for yourself.

Now that you've identified all the ingredients in the language soup of this sonnet, explore the sounds physically. As with your earlier work, let each sound of the sonnet move your body. Move from sound to sound, slowly at first and gradually building up to the speed of speaking. Let each sound make its own unique contribution. Let short sounds be short. Let long sounds be long. Let voiced sounds be voiced, voiceless sounds voiceless. Let plosive sounds be plosive and continuant sounds continue.

In almost any accent, these sonnets will challenge you to use your entire repertoire of sounds. Being aware of the density of sound in these sonnets can help you rise to the challenge of bringing all of yourself into speaking them. In one sonnet, the whole language in all of its pieces pours out of your gut, your mind, and your mouth.

Sonnet 117

ə ju   i   ʌ   æ aɪ   ɔ
ACCUSE ME THUS: THAT I HAVE SCANTED ALL

                ʊ   eɪ   ɚ
WHEREIN I SHOULD YOUR GREAT DESERTS REPAY,

      ɛ   ɒ(ɑ)
FORGET UPON YOUR DEAREST LOVE TO CALL,

        u
WHERETO ALL BONDS DO TIE ME DAY BY DAY;

              ɪ
THAT I HAVE FREQUENT BEEN WITH UNKNOWN MINDS,

                    oʊ
AND GIVEN TO TIME YOUR OWN DEAR-PURCHASED RIGHT;

          ɔɪ
THAT I HAVE HOISTED SAIL TO ALL THE WINDS

        a(æ)   ɑ
WHICH SHOULD TRANSPORT ME FARTHEST FROM YOUR SIGHT.

                                                aʊ
BOOK BOTH MY WILLFULNESS AND ERRORS DOWN,

AND ON JUST PROOF SURMISE ACCUMULATE;

BRING ME WITHIN THE LEVEL OF YOUR FROWN,

BUT SHOOT NOT AT ME IN YOUR WAKENED HATE;

SINCE MY APPEAL SAYS I DID STRIVE TO PROVE

THE CONSTANCY AND VIRTUE OF YOUR LOVE.

Sonnet 14

    ɒ(ɑ)   ə ɑ ʊ ɑɪ   ʌ
NOT FROM THE STARS DO I MY JUDGEMENT PLUCK,

     ɛ   ɪ   æ
AND YET METHINKS I HAVE ASTRONOMY;

              ʊ ɔ i
BUT NOT TO TELL OF GOOD OR EVIL LUCK,

    eɪ   ɝ
OF PLAGUES, OF DEARTHS, OR SEASONS' QUALITY;

       ɔ
NOR CAN I FORTUNE TO BRIEF MINUTES TELL,

  ɔɪ   ɚ
POINTING TO EACH HIS THUNDER, RAIN, AND WIND,

                 oʊ
OR SAY WITH PRINCES IF IT SHALL GO WELL

BY OFT PREDICT THAT I IN HEAVEN FIND.

BUT FROM THINE EYES MY KNOWLEDGE I DERIVE,

                  ɑ
AND, CONSTANT STARS, IN THEM I READ SUCH ART

        ju
AS TRUTH AND BEAUTY SHALL TOGETHER THRIVE

          aʊ

IF FROM THYSELF TO STORE THOU WOULD'ST CONVERT:

OR ELSE OF THEE THIS I PROGNOSTICATE,

THY END IS TRUTH'S AND BEAUTY'S DOOM AND DATE.

Sonnet 100

    ɛə ɑ   aʊ ju   æ   ɔ   oʊ ɔ
     ɛ
WHERE ART THOU MUSE, THAT THOU FORGET'ST SO LONG

  u   i   ɒ(ʌ)   ɪ   aɪ
TO SPEAK OF THAT WHICH GIVES THEE ALL THY MIGHT?

                       ɒ(ɑ) ʌ   ɝ
SPEND'ST THOU THY FURY ON SOME WORTHLESS SONG,

                        eɪ
DARK'NING THY POW'R TO LEND BASE SUBJECTS LIGHT?

RETURN FORGETFUL MUSE, AND STRAIGHT REDEEM

IN GENTLE NUMBERS TIME SO IDLY SPENT,

  u
SING TO THE EAR THAT DOTH THY LAYS ESTEEM,

AND GIVES THY PEN BOTH SKILL AND ARGUMENT.

RISE RESTY MUSE, MY LOVE'S SWEET FACE SURVEY.

IF TIME HAVE ANY WRINKLE GRAVEN THERE;

IF ANY BE A SATIRE TO DECAY

        ɔɪ
AND MAKE TIME'S SPOILS DESPISED EVERYWHERE.

        a (æ)
GIVE MY LOVE FAME FASTER THAN TIME WASTES LIFE;

                  ʊ
SO THOU PREVEN'ST HIS SCYTHE AND CROOKED KNIFE.

The Playwright's Use of Accents

    Playwrights such as Shakespeare, Shaw, and O'Neill created many characters with accents—digging into the playwright's sense of an accent will help you make choices about playing such characters. Sometimes sound changes for characters with accents are written into the dialogue of a play. For example, to suggest an Irish accent, Eugene O'Neill wrote the word DECENT as DACENT. This is called "eye-dialect."

Like many playwrights, O'Neill wrote a variety of accents in eye-dialect. His father, actor James O'Neill, was from the Irish province of Leinster. O'Neill's use of Irish sounds was no doubt influenced by the speech of relatives from that region. The sound changes suggested in the plays are characteristic of southern Irish speech in the vicinity of Dublin. Some of the accent features follow general, Irish pronunciation rules, others have a very limited application. The spellings fall short of detailed phonetic transcription and, taken completely literally, produce an obvious, hokey accent. However, if used as clues for subtler adjustments, they may help you to better serve the playwright's intent. Here are some examples of spellings O'Neill used to indicate an Irish accent. These spellings offer insight into his dramatic sense of Irish sounds. I will hazard a phonetic interpretation of each eye-dialect spelling.

O'Neill's Use of Irish Dialect Spelling
/ i / as in EASY to / e: /

easy/aisy	equal/aqual	eat/ate	beat/bate
beating/bating	decent/dacent	please/plaze	keep/kape
mean/mane	queer/quare	real/rale	sweet/swate
clean/clane	indeed/indade	beasts/bastes	decency/dacency
heathen/haythen			

/ ɛ / as in REST to / ɪ /

ever/ivir	every/ivery	heaven/hivin	gentlemen/gintlemin
forget/forgit	devil/divil	rest/rist	devilments/divilments
seven/sivin	them/thim	torment/tormint	went/wint
when/whin	again/agin	against/aginst	next/nixt
never/nivir	whatever/whativer		teakettle/teakittle

/ ə / of America turns to / i / America/Americy, Africa/Africy. Similarly, / oʊ / changes to / i / piano/piany, swallowed/swallyed.

/ oʊ / to / aʊ /	old/auld	hold/hauld	cold/cauld
/ ə / to / a /	society/sasiety		
/ ju / to / ji /	you/ye	you'd/ye'd	
/ ɪt / to / ʌt /	it/ut		
/ ʊ / to / ʌ /	would/wud	could/cud	
/ ʌ / to / a /	one/wan	up/ap	
/ aɪ / to / ɔɪ /	like/loike	pipe/poipe	time/toime
/ a / to / ar /	blast/blarst		
/ u / to / u: /	cruel/crool		
/ ɝ / to / ɔr /	sir/sorr		
/ t / to / t̪ /	matter/matther after/afther better/betther water/wather		

/ d / to / ð /	murder/murther
/ b / to / bʰ /	better/bhetter
/ d / to / d̪ /	drink/dhrink
/ tw / to / tj /	between/betune

Contractions:

These are some contractions that O'Neill uses to suggest the feel of the accent.

Contractions of IT:	'twas 'twasn't 'tis
Contractions of OF:	o'
Contractions of WILL:	'll bratts'll dagoes'll
Contractions of ISN'T:	aint

O'Neill changes IT / ɪt / to UT / ʌt / for an extreme accent. The speaker is Driscoll in *Bound East for Cardiff.*

"How cud ye doubt ut?"

The short vowel sound in could / kʊd / also changes to U / kʌd / in this example. This change can be used with SHOULD/WOULD as well.

The word blast / blæst / is spelled blarst / blɑrst / for Driscoll in *Bound East for Cardiff* and Burke in *Anna Christie.* This change could apply to certain other words in which the vowel / æ / is followed by consonants.

O'Neill sometimes spells O / oʊ / as AU / aʊ / which is regionally specific to the southeast. OLD / oʊld / is frequently spelled AULD / aʊld / and Nora in *A Touch of the Poet* says HAULD / haʊld / for HOLD / hoʊld /.

The words YOU / ju / and YOU'LL / jul / frequently become YE / ji / and YE'LL / jil /.

In *A Touch of the Poet*, Cregan adds H to the word DRINK. This is used rather than the more extreme TH sound, THRINK / ðrɪŋk / perhaps to keep the dialect more recognizable to the eye. But the subtler DH of DHRINK / d̪rɪŋk / is another sound peculiar to the Leinster region. BETTER is change to BHETTER. This change could indicate more breathiness. Cregan also uses D for TH in words like WITH and FATHER.

"To hell wid what his fader was!"

/ ð/ to / d /	with/wid	without/widout	father/fader

Some characters switch back and forth from using the full ING suffix / ɪŋ / to its IN' contrast / ɪn / . These switches may seem arbitrary but in some cases offer clues about what's going on with the character. For example, Carmody's dialect in *The Straw* is suggested almost entirely by dropping the G from the ING suffix.

"Ara don't be talkin'! That's no secret at all with the whole

town watchin' Eileen and you spoonin' together from the time
you was kids."

In Act III, however, Carmody is on his good behavior. Soberly visiting his sick daughter in the "sanitorium", he speaks with the full ING ending for the first time.

"Don't be talking of the trip.......You're not asking a bit of news from home."

He then reverts to IN' for the rest of the speech, which reads in part:

"He's always playin' hooky and roamin' the streets."

In a few plays, DARLING becomes DARLINT. And in *Bound East for Cardiff*, Driscoll changes SUDDEN to SUDDINT. This may indicate the speaker's sense of correctness.

The TION suffix is sometimes spelled SHUN / ʃʌn /. Driscoll is given this spelling for the words CONDITION and MENTION. In the word CONDITION, the spelling CONDISHUN would strengthen the stress of the third syllable. In the word MENTION, spelling it as MENSHUN eliminates the T sound.

BEEN is spelled BIN for Cregan in *More Stately Mansions*. This could be a contrast with the long British sound / bin / or with the / bɛn / pronunciation of some New Englanders.

"But I know how well your husband's bin doin' in his business."

Nora in *A Touch of the Poet* shortens KILLED to KILT. While Burke in *Anna Christie* lengthens DROWNED to DROWNDED. Norah, the "young Irish greenhorn" second girl in *Ah Wilderness*, turns HURT into a regular verb.

"O Glory be to God. Is it hurted you are?"

Paddy, in *The Hairy Ape* uses the long sound / i / rather than / ə / at the end of AMERICY and AFRICY. The spelling of society as sasiety for Carmody in *The Straw* may reflect the speaker's social attitudes.

In several plays, SIR is spelled SORR, not only changing the vowel, but also indicating a strong Irish R.

Part Five

The Plays

Introduction to the Plays

Playwright Gale Nelson was dramaturge at Trinity Rep where Anne Bogart called him "an eccentric thinker". As you read these plays you may agree.

The plays were written with one dominant sound in each scene and can be used in place of drill exercises.

Gale Nelson has this to say:

Writing *The Undiapered Filefish* and *Disciplining Dimes* within the context of a phonetically-driven system allowed plot to occur without planning by the author—rather plot was a symptom of language itself. That plot existed was neither expected nor discouraged. The plays are not intended to be anything more than plays; they would not exist, however without the playwright's having received fifty-eight lists of words for the completion of the project.

Gale Nelson's poetry titles are *Little Brass Pump* (Leave Books) and *stare decisis* (Burning Deck). A third title is forthcoming from Texture Press. A recipient of a Masters of Arts degree from the creative writing program at Brown University, Gale Nelson teaches poetry writing, playwriting, and literature courses at Brown, and previous taught at Trinity Repertory Conservatory. He is currently coordinator of Brown's Creative Writing program.

The Undiapered Filefish

A Play by Gale Nelson

Dramatis Personae

Jesse
Barbara
Abercrombe
Crane
Cath
Shemp
Todd
Phillip
Kittenface
Pesky
Randi
Barb
Stendahl

Scene / oʊ /

Jesse: Could you have KNOWN how OLD the TOAST is?

Barbara: The TOAST? The TOAST. GO on, SLOW the WHOLE meal with such queries as that.

Jesse: I'm serious

Barbara: I am too. It came from the new LOAF, you'll NOTE the use-by date.

Jesse: Fine, that date passed a week AGO.

Barbara: You never buy me what I need.

Jesse: Cut the PROLOGUE. I know you want a LOAD of OATS to make that GROTESQUE OKRA pound cake again. Is that it, love?

Barbara: GROTESQUE, you say?

Jesse: STOW the GROANS.

Barbara: DON'T PROFANE my counter with that kind of talk. What do you take our HOME for, a HOTEL? Do you think I run the bloody Ritz? Well, then, why didn't you find a BROCHURE by the bed?

Jesse: I TOLD you not to GOAD me.

Barbara: A MOTEL—that's your level. The Ritz, indeed. Where was I off to? You've never been inside a HOTEL.

Jesse: You're nothing but a SCOLD.

Barbara: I'm nothing is it?

Scene / a / or / æ /

Abercrombe: I'd RATHER BASK in the PATH of my PASTOR than fight a RAFT of NASTY bowls of chowder.

Crane: You've never been to FRANCE, sir.

Abercrombe: I'll make an EXAMPLE out of our DISASTER. I'll turn the DEMANDS into a DAFT list of FAST chatter.

Crane: A CHANT might be nice.

Abercrombe: A CHANT. A CHANT. Why, I CAN'T be thinking about the SLANT of each line to turn the chatter into music. That's you again, Crane, getting your head filled with DAFT ENCHANTMENTS.

Crane: I'd HALF like to LAUGH, sir, but AFTER tonight, things shall be a bit different.

Abercrombe: Don't MASK your meaning.

Crane: The STAFF is giving me a new TASK. I'm to MASTER the letters.

Abercrombe: That's always been up to BLANCHE.

Crane: She's not reliable, sir. She's been SLANTING the meaning of things. And the CASKET'S already been ASKED for.

Abercrombe: I'll DRAFT a letter, then.

Crane: Too late, sir. Our WRATH* SHAN'T be spared, shall not PASS, CAN'T be dismembered. We've orders from the CASTLE.

*/ ɔ / in British

Scene / ɚ /

Barbara: Don't come home for DINNER if there's not a GLIMMER of hope for us.

Jesse: The TENOR sings tonight. And the dancing OTTER is going on with the ACTOR from Down UNDER. It's all on the POSTER. And unless I am in ERROR, I've got two tickets in my pocket.

Barbara: The TENOR?

Jesse: And the OTTER.

Barbara: Oh the SILVER voice. That voice of VALOR. Oh thank you, LOVER.

Jesse: Mm. They've built a little RIVER on stage, the OTTER'S going to make a dam during the first act. With nothing but the PAPER from last week's programs. Imagine, all the WATER on the JASPER Lane THEATER boards.

Barbara: What'll we do for SUPPER?

Jesse: We'll go OVER to the edge of town and have a picnic. I'm going to CATER to your every wish, tonight.

Barbara: I hope it won't be too late to put the roast back in the ice box.

Jesse: If it's begun to thaw, it'll SOLDER itself to the side. We'll have it tomorrow.

Barbara: The TENOR, love. I hope they don't make him wear that DIAPER.

Jesse: In the last few days, he's been eating high-FIBER diet; he won't need the DIAPER. The OTTER'S got him eating tree branches.

Barbara: Where'd you hear such things?

Jesse: Saw it myself. They CENSOR the PAPERS. No one knows but us, and the OTTER, of course.

Barbara: Of course.

Scene / ɝ /

Cath: When that JERK LURKS in SEARCH of this collection of mollusks, I shall STIR his corn flakes.

Shemp: GIRL!

Cath: He'll BURN FERNS and LEARN to scat before he can shimmy in this SKIRT.

Shemp: GIRL!

Cath: Were he to SQUIRM free and PERFECT the CIRCLE, I'd still make him wheeze.

Shemp: GIRL, that's fine, but...

Cath: The MERCHANT of FUR can DETER you, but I've got the lozenge in my throat.

Shemp: GIRL, you've gone one direction farther this time.

Cath: I liked you better when you WERE as TERSE as the TURTLENECK you blended into.

Shemp: GIRL, that's enough.

Cath: HER SIR can INFER the SLUR from five hundred feet, honey. And you better watch your SHIRT.

Shemp: That's enough DIRT from your mouth, GIRL.

Cath: There's not a GERM in DIRT that can't PURR into the condominium of whiskers.

Scene / ɪɚ /
Todd: I HEAR you've got a contract.

Phillip: Don't SNEER at my contract, Todd.

Todd: No, I'm happy for you. I just want to CLEAR the air, buy you a BEER, sit around and chat.

Phillip: Well, I've seen too many SMEAR jobs, so if I APPEAR quick to my guard, I hope you'll understand.

Todd: I've been SPEARED by the critics enough times to know where you're coming from.

Phillip: So I've heard.

Todd: The last thing I would want is for you to feel like I want to hurt you. I'm interested in your CAREER.

Phillip: Thanks, Todd. I've had to rub my nose in lots of REARS to get where I am.

Todd: I know what you're saying. A reputation is a QUEER thing, so I've been one to STEER away from anything that might seem unseemly.

Phillip: I've always respected you, Todd. You're NEAR the top of this profession. And you've got a really good EAR for the line.

Todd: I think you're first TIER, too, Phillip. I'm glad to think of you as my PEER.

Phillip: Well, I've got a contract, Todd.

Todd: We both know you've browned your nose for it, though. And my nose is clean.

Phillip: When I HEAR the phrase mini-wear, I conjure a picture of a skinny bear, angry and looking for trouble. But when I mention to you that I've got a tape of

DEER running for cover, what do you think?

Todd: That it's time to escape?

Scene / ɛɚ /

Abercrombe: When the CHAIR is encircled by the spiritual sphere, do we DARE to revolve in our plastered-down HAIR

Crane: I SHARE your interest in the philosophical, sir, but WHERE might this lead us?

Abercrombe: Into the advanced beat of conservation, the SCARE of rabbits to SPARE but no PAIR SHARING the same chromosomes.

Crane: I don't follow, sir.

Abercrombe: The LAIR, Crane. How might we FARE if only RARE specimens of HARE are preserved?

Crane: This is not our mission, sir. The castle has asked us to look for the SCARCE MARES of the region and CARE for them.

Abercrombe: THEIR message was imbedded in the letter. If you SQUARE the value of each letter and look for whole words in the product, mastering the process in a linear manner, don't STARE Crane, you know this system has been used by the castle for three decades.

Crane: So, you know.

Abercrombe: I can also tell you the double-encoded message. "AIR on FAIR waters" comes to tell us that France is evergreen and yellow the passage between our elms.

Crane: No, sir. France provides passage-way forever when we've eliminated the bell-tower.

French Scene One

This scene features shared French/English words. The scene can be read using a range of pronunciation from very French to a less extreme contrast with American English. Below are exmaples of the different types of words used in this scene.

tion ending - nat*ion*	sion ending - pas*sion*	ible ending - terr*ible*
an ending - urb*an*	en ending - happ*en*	ance ending - d*ance*
ment ending - experi*ment*	ant ending - import*ant*	im prefix - *im*pose
in prefix - *in*trude	en prefix - *en*tire	ial ending - mater*ial*
con prefix - *con*jure		

Kittenface: I'm sorry you have to go.

Pesky: Let the formation of our nation's cause be blindfolded to the gestation process.

Kittenface: The connection is silly--we are here to discuss the damnation of truth in commencement scaffolds.

Pesky: I do have to go.

Kittenface: Let the ball roll, though. Give in to association, the formation of which only blackened tiles could forgive.

Pesky: That's the terrible predicament. Fashion persists. Discretion is made possible through abdication of love.

Kittenface: That's admirable. A turban of even-numbered progressions; absurd.

Pesky: Look, we'll continue this conversation later. Stiffen the upper lip, deepen your growl, and make impossible demands from the tenor.

Kittenface: Deepen your meaning.

Pesky: Maintain discretion. The incredible things that are going to happen if they come into the confession would open the valise entirely.

Kittenface: Is this possible?

Pesky: Even likely.

Kittenface: We'll send for the chicken, then.

Pesky: Have the chicken feign compassion. Let them think us to be urban, formidable.

Kittenface: And our obsessions will stiffen into silence.

Scene / ɑɚ /
Todd: Don't SCARF the potatoes.

Phillip: ARSON.

Todd: DARN you, Phillip, don't turn this HEARTH bare.

Phillip: I need some STARCH.

Todd: They'll CHARGE me double if we keep eating.

Phillip: And I've got a contract.

Todd: That's a FARCE. Not even worth a rat's ass.

Phillip: Too small for my face.

Todd: You'd have to ARCH your back, Phillip. You could do it.

Phillip: ARCH it? I'd have to double over. MARCH into the world of micro-organisms, SHARPEN my knowledge of molecular science and shudder.

Todd: All from SCARFING too many potatoes. So, you see my point.

Phillip: ARSON. I'll burn this barn to the ground if they over CHARGE you.

Todd: That'll keep our reputations clear.

Phillip: Don't ARCH your back, Todd.

Todd: It's my brow I've got ARCHED. So you see, this isn't a FARCE. Take it easy on the spuds.

Scene / ɔɚ /
Barbara: PORK ORGANS.

Jesse: FOR supper?

Barbara: It's all we could AFFORD, unless you'd like to take on a second MORT-GAGE.

Jesse: My FORK won't dip into PORK ORGANS.

Barbara: That's what's in STORE for us tonight, love.

Jesse: It's real PORK, I hope.

Barbara: Well, actually, it's not quite NORMAL.

Jesse: Not quite NORMAL?

Barbara: It's from that SWARM of WART hogs that TORE through town last week when the FORMAL dance was SORT of winding down.

Jesse: WART hog FOR supper. Love, what has gotten into you?

Barbara: I've begun to baste it with PORT wine. Or would you prefer the full es-sence of PORK ORGANS?

Jesse: I can't take any MORE of this. And to think the otter has left town. POUR me a PORT, would you, love?

Barbara: And leave the PORK ORGANS?

Jesse: Next you'll be telling me that you were daft enough to buy some MORE of those SORTED STORK patties.

Barbara: We were running SHORT.

Scene / ʊɚ /

Stendahl: The POOR ASSURE the necessity of our plans. We cannot be DOUR, but properly discreet in our adventures. For it is in love and hate that we can discern the OBSCURE emotions that have been sent heavenward, and, in this mind, TOUR the streets and the SEWERS below to our heart's content. This then SECURE, what have we to say but that the noble act of love is putrid, the ALLURE of aftershave, a twentieth century twist on the unnatural will to ENDURE class struggle when the LURE of rising through hard work and PURE heart is never enough to empower the lazy branches of the BUREAUCRACY, those BOORS who have no home but the office, no ALLURE but the pencil sharpener, no PURE thoughts but of changing from form 3 dash 2 7 1 1 to the more pernicious 3 dash 2 7 1 1 A. The necessity of our plans is ASSURED by the increasing POOR. And I shall be the certain slant of sunlight that bears down into their retinas.

Scene / aɪɚ /

Cath: Don't REQUIRE me to INQUIRE about who you ADMIRE. I can't PERSPIRE over every rock- encrusted SIRE.

Shemp: Girl. . .

Cath: Could you hand me the hair DRYER? Prior to today, I'd have said you were just a DIRE case, but now, honey, I ADMIRE how you never TIRE of trying to find the right ATTIRE. But joining a church CHOIR?

Shemp: I like to sing.

Cath: I like to bring the raft to the spring and roll through the BRIAR when the WIRE to WIRE EMPIRE can't go any HIGHER. And I like to read a path of stones when the blood has come from your telephone, but you don't see me joining the church CHOIR.

Shemp: I.

Cath: HIRE yourself a SQUIRE and see what MIRE you two can construe, but don't come to me with the first three songs about Moses and the burning BRIAR. That PYRE LIAR was out to gore the other means to INSPIRE, then RETIRE.

Shemp: You've no idea what you're saying.

Cath: Yeah, but you're the one who will have to address the tenors wearing a robe.

Scene / ɔɪɚ /

Crane: The LAWYER is pulling up.

Abercrombie: When the LAWYER crosses the FOYER, mechanize.

Crane: Yes, sir. Our EMPLOYERS at the castle will be rather keen to have the tapes, no doubt.

Abercrombe: Whenever a LAWYER can go this long without leaving some bit of scorched earth, we may be sure that he's not quite the DESTROYER we've made him out to be.

Crane: The FOYER is prepared. SAWYER will meet the LAWYER at the door. They're moving into the FOYER. They're below the chandelier.

Abercrombe: Has SAWYER got the weathervane in sight?

Crane: No, his back's to it. The LAWYER must have the cue from somewhere in the team.

Abercrombe: What I wouldn't give for the FOYER bell-pull routine we used to run in the last decade. The ruse was a stunner.

Crane: But the otter made it a bit outdated, wouldn't you say?

Abercrombe: Let us see if the LAWYER gives us anything. I'm betting that SAWYER will let him leave the FOYER without getting the least bit first.

Crane: If that's the case, the otter plan will be the DESTROYER of weeks of careful ruse- building. Sir, what could we do?

Abercrombe: We could engage the weathervane against the castle's instructions. That would be my first step.

Crane: They're shaking hands. SAWYER is saying little nothings. The LAWYER is leaving through the FOYER door, nothing said. Should we move in?

Abercrombe: Too late. The weathervane undercut by otter plans. What could be more demoralizing?

Scene / aʊɚ /
Barbara: I was just about to SCOUR the SHOWER curtain when you came in.

Jesse: I went shopping. That FLOUR you've been using to make bread is horrible. Here's some fresh FLOUR for you. And some daisies.

Barbara: What lovely FLOWERS. Jesse, you're a dear.

Jesse: Just didn't want you to GLOWER about throwing out the old FLOUR.

Barbara: You're a love.

Jesse: And I vow to begin to make my own salads.

Barbara: Just because I put sour dressing on by mistake?

Jesse: No, I'm a changed man. The FLOUR'S not just for you to make bread. Why, some day I'll make a loaf.

Barbara: Just after you fix the toilet. Or buy me a car with POWER steering. You and your promises. The only ones that ever come true have something to do with the entertainment HOUR.

Jesse: We've made the theater OUR little home away from home, that's true, but if I had the POWER to do everything, I'd do it just like that. Why should you have to SCOUR that old curtain. We'll take SHOWERS with it for another six years if I don't do something. That's it. I'm going downtown to buy a new SHOWER curtain.

Barbara: But, lover, I've just SCOURED it. Wait a few weeks, so I'll feel as though my effort went for good use. Not an HOUR wasted.

Jesse: Then, we'll queue up for tickets for the tenor. What a POWERFUL voice, you always say.

Barbara: I haven't been GLOWERING the past two weeks just to hear that tenor again.

Jesse: But the tenor's going to be our little treat.

French Scene Two
This scene is a continuation of the shared French/English words from page 134

Pesky: You are, then, a student of imitation?

Kittenface: The material you relate conflicts with the event.

Pesky: We've got a tape. You infamous imposter, converting yourself into the position of confidant.

Kittenface: The chicken was too discontent to be prudent. The stance I took was that I could intrude the event, misrepresent the conflict, and flee. I saw no need to confer.

Pesky: The ethereal engine of trance.

Kittenface: For us to seem innocent, I had to prance and dance through an inferno of bugs. Not one could impair us, engulf us, or conjure a clue to the conflict. Don't ask me to repent. I advance our cause, enthrall the enemy with intelligent ruse, and you congregate the facts around the manner I implement is to impose impolite rot in the face of an advantageous play, important this advantage.

Pesky: The entire imperial force wishes to condemn us, finance a counter-insurrection, and you ask me to congratulate?

Kittenface: Yes.

Pesky: You impetuous infant. You consort to vanity. You engine of romance. You kittenfaced discontent of self-designed import. You conduct your resources as confident commandant, yet you ornament yourself as needing to repent nothing, impose nothing, convert nothing, but smarty-pant words.

Kittenface: The entire ensemble could inform you of no less. Yet I saved the day. We did an experiment with the chicken, and the impetuous nature informed us indirectly to constrict activities. I advanced us in my engaging in the double-talk. So augment my team. But, you may go now.

Scene / r /
This scene features / r / between vowels.

Stemdahl: The petite SIRAH goes well with any lighter dish, but the HEROIC pinot NOIR IS more VIRILE, nearly FURRY going to down, but a LIFTER OF the SPIRIT in the glass. A TERRIBLE, BERRY cabernet sauvignon can BURROW into the HEROIC SURRENDER AND WORRY the BORING CHORUS of chablis- drinking CONQUERORS with COURAGE in their hearts and on their tongues. The HILARITY of it all. Not even a thought to the sauvignon blanc, which may PERISH if we TARRY from its CORNER OF the cellar, hidden behind the DRAPERY, becoming a MIRROR IMAGE of the ARID land on which it thrives. Ah, the CHEERY CHERRY FLAVORING of the zinfandel, a STORY in its ORIGINS to be sure, but an ARIA for the palate. The LYRIC mood unleashed when the FURY is set to WORRY about the grapes, the ORALLY ingested feast for the TORRID night of pulling corks from magnums, let our MORALS fall aside for one brief HOUR, AND suffer nothing less than the finest bottle of them all, the one we dare not touch FOR AGE is still, even now, on its side, OVER A hundred years and still MATURING, still above the fray, still HEROIC in its tannic acid, let us sip from it before we bow our heads for day upon week upon decade before this VERY vestige of OUR ANCESTRY. Damn the poor, damn the hope we build, drink this wine, make MERRY, BURROW into the heart of CHARACTERISTICS known by a wink and a sigh, and gasp at the blood-like hue of this dynastic wine, titanically holding forth upon our minds.

Scene / u / *or* / ju /
Abercrombe: Penguin upstarts, I tell you.

Crane: The NUDE TUNA is droning on, a TUNE I ASSUME YOU know, DUE to the few LUMINESCENT RETINUE left in this area.

Abercrombe: Not one long-nosed filefish left in COSTUME, and we in PURSUIT of upstart penguins.

Crane: But we have gathered in the lobster in Whitman's beard.

Abercrombe: That old COSTUME. An ILLUSION played out on CUE with every DUPE, every TUNIC ready to burst buttons. And the tuxedo blistering my chest, my chest, mind YOU, with only a penguin to RESUME the DUTIFUL ice CUBE dance.

Crane: I have the VOLUMINOUS citings of the lobstering DUTY, sir.
Abercrombe: The plate turns to glass, and only the ears remain.

Crane: A glass-bottom boat for lobster surveillance!

Abercrombe: Those little blue longnose filefish are coming; not the same thing, mind YOU, as a long- nosed filefish, which is a normal filefish with a nose somewhat longer than USUAL. No, a true longnose filefish pays its DUES. It sprouts a snout of heroic proportions. While the Picasso triggerfish makes me hear the TUNA LUTE TUNE as though the penguins went back to the Antarctic Circle.

Crane: We've seen ingenuity in our day, but too NUMEROUS are the TULIPS for me to decipher.

Abercrombe: I shall TUTOR you, Crane; I shall EXHUME the body of the lacerated osteopath and render a DUTIFUL STUDENT of YOU. The penguin upstarts will CONSUME my last days on the force, I can see that already. But the DUKE can't get me to turn in my TUNIC below the tuxedo without a fight. And you'll have earned your mesh-ground platter when I'm done with YOU, Crane. Upstart penguins, indeed!

Scene / æ /

Randi: I've reports from Crane that they've ignored the CRAB DAM altogether.

Barb: Are they MAD?

Randi: THAT, I'll THANK you to be reminded is a TAG they CAN wear all the time.

Barb: They've BABBLED about all sorts of ANGLES.

Randi: I RANG the LAD, and he used LANGUAGE as though it were AN AX.

Barb: The CACKLE TRAP, speaking from a VAN, no doubt.

Randi: A CAB. CAN you believe THAT?

Barb: They are not to be trusted.

Randi: Crane's done some good work recently, ABERCROMBIE, however, ever since he and ALBERT stopped CHATTING, and when he lost the NAB, he's been APT to FABRICATE his suspicions as though he wrote ROMANCE novels.

Barb: Crane MAPPED out this LAMB and RAT TRAP, I'll HAVE you remember.

Randi: It worked better THAN the otter SLAB.

Barb: And what of the tenor, getting FAT eating nothing but GALLON upon GALLON of brickle ice cream.

Randi: We've got to get him to take the APPLE pie seriously if we want to replace the SHABBY work the field team is doing.

Barb: So, we're in the same CAMP.

Randi: With the RABBIT and the CACTUS branch.

Scene / aʊ /

Cath: HOW can a COW ROUSE the hen HOUSE? I'll tell you, Shemp. By GROUND-ING the NOW-CROWD into a drool. The crust in a MOUTH is a HOWL when a CROWN comes loose in a TOWN with no dentist.

Shemp: HOW can you say that?

Cath: The LOUNGE is full of skulls, waiting to PLOW through SOUND. And the OWL stays up late when fate can grate AROUND here.

Shemp: The SOUNDS you come up with.

Cath: Did I SHROUD the PROUD in CLOUD nine protrusions?

Shemp: Girl, you did.

Cath: Then, let's MOUTH the words to the new disco birds, and HOWL.

Shemp: I'm up for that, but I'm PROUD of our HOUSE, too.

Cath: Then let's play for clay, and run with the sun, but when the OWL comes to life, PLOW the floor with our first thirty-three COW-BROWN eye-contact delights.

Shemp: But Cath...

Cath: In the fifth row of seas we'll be selling stocks and bonds of lariats.

Scene / ɔ /

Crane: They BOUGHT the bit of WALL at the AUCTION.

Abercrombe: How much did it run?

Crane: They SAW to an early CALL. Little more than budget.

Abercrombe: I THOUGHT we'd really get into the red this time.

Crane: Let's just hope the STRAW surrounding the device won't FLAW the sound quality too much.

Abercrombe: When will the vehicle carrying the WALL arrive?

Crane: DAWN. The AUTO had been CHALK-ASSAULTED by the local traffic commission, so they were held over until they paid their parking fines.

Abercrombe: Nothing's ever a WALTZ, is it?

Crane: They'll still be here before the otter arrives.

Abercrombe: We'll stash it in the VAULT until the otter has been briefed. Wouldn't want to JAW about it without everyone WALKING by the same set of quicksand.

Crane: The WALL had been SCRAWLED on, we're told.

Abercrombe: May be a message.

Crane: "AUDIENCE SAW GAUNT puffin PAW at toast."

Abercrombe: I read that as "the shadow puppet play is nearing completion."

Crane: I concur.

Scene / ɑ / *or* / ɒ /

Stendahl: WHAT COMEDY, this NOD to the POSSIBLE INVOLVEMENT of GOD is the religion of the ODD COLLEGE SCHOLAR. Or is it tragedy? For the SOLID idea CANNOT be scorned just because the DOT above the 'i' has flip-FLOPPED into the shape of Christmas HOLLY. The courage is there, yet the humor begins to become a JOLLY MODEL for us to ROB. The TONGS heat up as as though we've been to see the DONKEY. What POSSIBLE manner of whiskers could be given to MOP this recliner, what shattering tape, SCOTCH or otherwise, could bind the will of these putrid few who have never GOLFED in snow? There is the MODEL to FOLLOW through the time known only as eternity. TOP that with a DOLLAR donation, rise ON the wings of a MOTH-eaten cape that has never been cleansed in marmalade.

German Scene One

This scene contains a high concentration of sounds which contrast in an American and German accent.

Pesky: We seem to want you to equal the swim between trains.

Kittenface: Dwell on this—the twelve Swiss tenors wore dwarf suits that twinned them.

Pesky: Let's wage love. Let's sweat between sheets, let's swell with one another, woo one another, wait for ways to assuage fear.

Kittenface: You make me twitch.

Pesky: Let us exchange clothes. The blue pants fit you better.

Kittenface: Wait. We don't have to be so swift—we've had our times, it's true, but also our differences. And I wonder how love would bestow a new swarm of feelings.

Pesky: Stop waxing poetical, Kittenface. Dwell heart inside heart with me, twinkle your eyes when we entwine. Delight in wonder with me, as I should do with you.

Kittenface: A wall remains between my head and my body.

Pesky: Then swim between trains instead. Forget the Swiss dwarf tenors, the otter, the filefish lettuce, at least for a sweet, sweat-released day and night and day again—for as long as light flashes upon our souls, and we don't waste away our entrails.

Kittenface: Then I am yours.

Scene / ɔɪ /

Barbara: You've got to make a CHOICE, love. Either SPOIL the BOY, or make him a man.

Jesse: Just because I brought home a TOY for the tyke doesn't mean you have to raise your VOICE.

Barbara: What about the COIN?

Jesse: The POINT is he's just a tyke.

Barbara: He's SPOILT, love.

Jesse: He's not. He makes NOISE with the BOYS on the next block, he JOINS them in game after game with that vile COIL of rope. How often does he come home a mess, you ráving about the SOIL he tracks in.

Barbara: And what do you do? Give him a gift.

Jesse: And me, bringing you gifts from the market, do you say I'm SPOILING you, too?

Barbara: Thanks for the pint of SOY I asked for, which I can't even use tonight since I decided to BROIL the fish.

Jesse: No, love. Do it up right, in a little sesame OIL. A big stack of MOIST rice, a gravy made of JOINTS of beef, a JOY to have on my tongue. Like what you did last night.

Barbara: I made lasagna last night.

Jesse: Last week, then, when we had our CHOICE of liver or SOY-based chops with mold-infested toast.

Barbara: The BOY, love. We've lost sight of the BOY.

Jesse: He'll be fine, just you wait and see.

Scene / aɪ /

Abercrombe: That MIME is VILE, Crane.

Crane: I thought you MIGHT LIKE him. He's one of NINE agents we could FIND with such skills.

Abercrombe: No STYLE at all, though. How can he tip us off if he hears something?

Crane: SIGN language. He's helped us nab a SLIME taking a BRIBE, he worked with a group of BRINE to bring down the SPY ring in TIGHT pants.

Abercrombe: Really? I wanted that ASSIGNMENT. BIKE pants BILE, MY goodness. He was on your SIDE for that case?

Crane: We went WILD with his help, why the guild stopped FRYING our fish for a month after that case.

Abercrombe: Even the otter kept himself in check, going the extra MILE, nearly keeping his tail DRY. All of these cases, Crane, and the MIME was in on them?

Crane: We had him WRITE down everything after, when the TIME was RIGHT, we put the material into the FILE, everything on the up and up.

Abercrombe: So the MIME is in LINE. I've a MIND to consider the fixtures CHIDE as too SLY, though. I know he was on that case, SMILING at every troubadour who came for the fish-FRY.

Crane: That was years ago.

Abercrombe: VILE, though, simply VILE.

Crane: He won't even wink at the bee HIVE, now, sir. He's one of our best men.

Abercrombe: I'll work with him for AWHILE, see what comes from his corner.

Scene / i /

Stendahl: You may begin to look for MOTIFS within this work. The MEAL that Jesse and Barbara prepare. The THIEF, or other ILLEGAL activity that SEEMS to take place. WE'D trust the WHEEZING Abercrombe, or do we CLEAVE to the side of Crane? Might WE BELIEVE they are both in NEED of a LEADER, someone WE might BE more readily able to recognize as BEING like a PRIEST? HE'LL tell all, you're thinking, this Stendahl. He'll SCREAM the bloody plot, WE'LL FEEL CHEATED, unable to come to APPRECIATE the work on our own terms. FREE to SHIELD yourselves from my DEEP but MEEK IDEAS. I shall conjure something else, then. We are here not to PLEASE each other, but for you to LEASE your attention to us for a particular period, say THREE WEEKS, a handful of seconds, a day, the length of a SCREAM, COMPLETELY, forever, until the COMPLETION of this play. And the play's ALLE-

GIANCE—is it with FIENDS, the castle QUEEN, what has been REVEALED SEEMS more a DREAM than a SIEGE. And that is what I must convey, that the MEANING is not found by READING the program, looking at the CEILING, FREEING your legs from their cramped position beneath your SEAT; the LEAF upon LEAF of paper used to write this play is not before you, literally, only the words. This is your PEEK behind the curtain, your moment to FEEL the play was AGREEABLE to making your enjoyment primary, but the GREEDY actors wish to return, give lines again that you shall distill well beyond the fathoming FEMUR of the director, who has wanted all this time to APPEASE you by giving a PASTICHE of show tunes instead.

Scene / ɪ /

Cath: I'm HIP to the GLIB gab of BEING by the MILL, but WILL the CHIN CONVINCE?

ShemP: Yes.

Cath: Can I BRING THIS STRING to the PRINCE and RIG a CLIP to SINK HIS GIN?

Shemp: From what I've seen.

Cath: I can't be serious, FIGURING a SLICK LITTLE duck can STILL get the IMAGE right, TICKLE the tongue and RIPPLE the fun. But IF I'm not QUICK, then the FIG WILL be blowing a fife, and IN the LITTLE LIMBER scene, I'll be BRILLIANT.

Shemp: You WILL KILL them all. The PRINCE, the WIDOW, the otter, even the SHIP full of LIMP-WRISTED haddocks.

Cath: SWIM through THIS ILL-timed number and I'll be making a VIDEO WITH all the TRICKS IN the book to CONVINCE ENGLAND that I'm the ILK for them.

Shemp: You can BRING IT off, Cath.

Cath: I'll be BIG, I'll be the HIP THING for a week, then change my WIG and BUILD a new BEING.

Shemp: They'll swallow the GARLIC PILL, Cath.

Cath: And that WILL RING me IN.

Scene / eɪ /

Phillip: THEY haven't given us much notice for awhile.

Todd: THEY better not SAY THEY GAVE us our fair share.

Phillip: Who do THEY think they are? I gave my best audition, I did it for my mother's SAKE, and the RAGE that is building in my heart.

Todd: MAYBE THEY'LL give us a NAKED scene LATER on.

Phillip: THEY'LL FADE the lights knowing this crowd. The PRAISE I could have TRADED on, the FAME, the love, my ability to AMAZE them.

Todd: Don't forget that it could be our GAIN if the PLAY FADES.

Phillip: True. What if THEY CLAIM us as the only ones to SAY our lines with joy, with emphasis, with diction.

Todd: THEY'LL GAUGE us better if we can TRADE on our brooding PLACE on this fetid TABLE.

Phillip: For the WAGE I'm earning, they better BEHAVE toward me.

Todd: At least you've a contract. THEY move like so many SNAILS when dealing with me. I MADE the GRADE. I wore the CAPE in that fiasco last year, and I'll SKATE through this yet.

Phillip: This is our PLAY, MADE for us, to shine through when all else seems to STALE.

Todd: We won't APE their lines next time.

Phillip: You, MAYBE, but my nose has been bloodied once too often. I'm no longer apt to be TAMED.

Todd: I won't STAY if you won't.

Phillip: The SAME here.

Scene / ε /
Crane: The coral polyps are in JEOPARDY.

Abercrombe: AGAIN? Too MANY triggerfish, if you ask me.

Crane: Shall I GET the NET? I could put TOGETHER a KETTLE of THEM by FEBRUARY. And we could keep THEM under the BED.

Abercrombe: They're a WEAPON only WHEN they're WET, not when they go BELLY up.

Crane: But the polyp BECKONS THEM, and THEN the PHLEGM will WELL up.

Abercrombe: I GUESS we'll have to do something. But we need the triggerfish if we have ANY chance to WHET the actor's appetite for our METHOD.

Crane: He SAID that the TEPID water would be EXCELLENT.

Abercrombe: DEAF ears. I'm turning DEAF ears, Crane. TEPID water, indeed. How might we maintain our stock of filefish?

Crane: Go to the HELM AGAIN, DEFEND THEM from our adversary.

Abercrombe: I can't go on buying LETTUCE every time our filefish are THREAT-ENED by the damn actor and his TEPID water. What do they say at the castle?

Crane: The PECKING order has been reversed.

Abercrombe: They SAID that? We should have LEFT the force WHEN we had the chance. Now our filefish and triggerfish are confined as though they FELL under a HEX. We'll have them GUEST-conducting the Amsterdam Symphony Orchestra at this rate.

Crane: That FELL through, sir. But we've still got TEN polyp samples in a HEN.

Abercrombe: My SENSE is that we've got to FELL the HEN, THEN.

Crane: VERY WELL, sir.

Scene / ɑ /

Phillip: I've studied KARATE, worked in a GARAGE, eaten the great clam dips of the Midwest.

Todd: I did SPA work in the PLAZA, and found myself among the SUAVEST FATHERS in the town.

Phillip: You were a FAÇADE, a SUAVE. You couldn't even tell a TACO from a tortilla.

Todd: I've never mistaken a vicuna for a LLAMA, though.

Phillip: That was ten years ago, and I was translating the Argentine PSALM into a poetic rendition.

Todd: You're no MACHO cuspid-bulging bastion.

Phillip: I can tell you more than a few things about this PALM SAGA, though.

Todd: BLAH, BLAH, BLAH. Try to remain a black-belt KARATE king pin, just try.

Phillip: I'd CALM down if I were you.

Todd: I thought we had agreed not to fight. Here you are, raising your voice.

Phillip: You're the last MACHO LLAMA herder I'll ever trust.

Todd: That's what they all say.

Phillip: I think you're waiting for me to show you how the PALM of my hand feels driven into your cheek.

Todd: SUAVE GARAGE attendant, that's all I've got to say.

Scene / ʌ /

Barbara: I'm trying to make FUDGE brownies, and you COME home with DOUBLE-DUNK MONKFISH GUM.

Jesse: And a MUG of MUD pie, LOVE, JUST for you.

Barbara: You'll make the HUNK of FUDGE brownies seems like so MUCH JUNK food.

Jesse: My TRUCK is full of CUB SUDS, and the YOUNG know where the TRUNK key is. They'll be AMONG the BUG-SUCKING BLOOD samples before you'll finish that batch.

Barbara: You didn't get STUNG by the DUCK-HUGGING UNCLE, did you?

Jesse: You sting my pride. Of course his FLOOD of UTTERLY-failed attempts were obvious to me. I've HUNG out with the otter, you know.

Barbara : What I wouldn't give to hear the tenor again.

Jesse: He's a CHUM, too. I'll RUN into town later and bring him home. After he's SUNG for the SONS of tree bark society. They're a bit of a DUMB lot, they asked for RUM when everyone knows we've got this great store of sauternes.

Barbara: Until then, might we CUDDLE UP, talk about the boy?

Jesse: What have I DONE for the boy this time?

Barbara: NOTHING. He's your SON, though, and I should think you'd want to see if he's having enough FUN.

Jesse: I just make sure he's not hanging out with those PUGS in the SLUMS, and I listen to his records about insect legs.

Barbara: He's taking after you, I think.

German Scene 2

This is a continuation of the contrasts explored in German Scene One.

Pesky: The queen is wondering which of us to squash.

Kittenface: We can't quit, though, even if the wheel points our way.

Pesky: Should we square off, where should we meet?

Kittenface: The Alps. We can quell their motor van with equine shadows.

Pesky: Of course, the farm. Equal parts quiet and resolve.

Kittenface: The squirrel can swim through with supplies. The horses are squired, and the white one is speedy.

Pesky: Are the dwarf contingencies there?

Kittenface: Not while on tour. It should square us up nicely, should the queen turn.

Pesky: We've got to get the triggerfish wheat--can you squeeze the mime?

Kittenface: No, the mime's turned against us. We'll have to sequester the chicken and pray for the best.

Pesky: We'll make it to the Alps, won't we?

Kittenface: The chicken always said we would end up there, tending to bovines and equines. The sweet grass to lie in, the long days of planning our return, our courting the queen from afar to shift the castle's goals once again. All twinned with you, Pesky.

Pesky: I know.

Kittenface: We've been through a lot, but the quest continues to grow in directions we couldn't anticipate. We dwindle our hopes and love emerges. We wage war on the otter, and the queen condemns us. But we'll have the Alps. And we'll get a triggerfish supply--and bells for the cows. Brass bells.

Pesky: And I'll swim every summer eve with you.

Scene / ə /

Randi: I do not AGREE with your ACCOUNT of the ATTACK.

Barb: It's what the otter observed. I was AMUSED by his ATTEMPT to OBSCURE the filefish involvement, but he was ATTUNED to your mind to APPEAL to that source.

Randi: He'd do it AGAIN, too, that otter. ADIEU to him, that's what I say. AMONG the thirty ACCOUNTS UPON Crane and Abercrombe's project. I would say his was THE least ABOVE-board.

Barb: I found it the most able to keep AFLOAT all THE details.

Randi: What of THE mime's?

Barb: I am UNAFFECTED by THE mime, ALAS. They say THE mime is quite AGREE-ABLE.

150

Randi: THE mime is going to OBJECT to our going with the otter's ACCOUNT.

Barb: THE queen wants those two to fry for the filefish fiasco, and this will not AMUSE her, this APPEAL.

Randi: THE filefish are fine, though, aren't they?
Barb: And THE triggerfish. But THE hen's been felled for the want of polyp samples.

Randi: THE queen will send them AFLOAT this time. Until their unit is gone, we'll have to go AGAIN and AGAIN, to explain every project, and to rely on that otter seems OBJECTIONABLE.

Barb: It is THE best ACCOUNT, though. You do AGREE?

Randi: Okay, but you're going to run this AFFAIR.

Scene / ʊ /
Jesse: Where's my GOOD COOK hiding her SUGAR supplies?

Barbara: You're not going to get your HOOKS into my SUGAR.

Jesse: But I've brought home the WOOD PUDDING, and it needs a bit more SUGAR.

Barbara: COULD you use the GOOD substitute instead?

Jesse: The substitute? On WOOD PUDDING! The BOOK tells us quite clearly that WOOD PUDDING needs SUGAR, and lots of it.

Barbara: Well, I hid it behind the WOOL PULLOVERS. In case a CROOK were to come in, LOOKING for valuables.

Jesse: I STOOD on the step ladder and it turns out to be below the sink, with those God-awful PULLOVERS.

Barbara: If you WOULD like, I'll pour you a glass of wine.

Jesse: I TOOK the port off the dining room table on the way in.

Barbara: That's for show. I hid the real port in the breakfast NOOK.

Jesse: Do you want to hear the tenor tonight?

Barbara: I've been thinking that we've gone to hear the tenor quite often recently. Do you have a thing going with that otter?

Jesse: Love! SUGAR! I STOOD at the altar with you, and I'll be nuzzling my COOK for the rest of my days.

Scene / u /

Stendahl: It is TRUE, then, that YOU'VE been watching CLUE after CLUE come bristling through the fog of language, and now the road is nearly fully behind YOU. Don't BROOD. CHEW on the significance of each scene, each character. Ask yourself WHO DREW YOU in, WHO seemed to fail the test of empathy. Was there a PRUDE among the GROUP? Was there TOO much talk of filefish, at the expense of the TUNA, the walrus and the pork entrails? Would the PLUME of YOUTH have been better served by attending the follies shown next door? Was the CRUDE COSTUMING INTRUSIVE? Would you stand for a second act? WHO would YOU DOODLE were you Hirschfield? If the play GREW on YOU, and YOU are now feeling the tingling sensation that comes to BLOOM in the best of performances, the KUDOS are DUE to the actors, the set designer, the fellows WHO SCREW in the lights, but not to the POODLE WHO would not deign to be part of this mess. And the greatest NOUGAT that YOU may gnaw at THROUGH the weeks to come—this speech has come before the last. Your sense of closure is RUINED, in advance. I DREW YOU in, SPOON-fed YOU ideas, and what is left to DO? Sit THROUGH the last few scenes, applaud, politely, and claim it on your income tax. Call it post- primordial OOZE, or GOO. They'll believe YOU. They'll want your ticket stub, however, so don't leave it in your pocket when you send your SUIT to the cleaners.

Special Pronunciations

This scene features words that are usually pronounced differently in British and USA English.

Todd: We've BEEN left out AGAIN. EITHER we demand our rights, or we steal the show.

Phillip: NEITHER, Todd. My NEPHEW tells me that we've been followed throughout by a CLERK.

Todd: Not the fellow wearing the DERBY.

Phillip: He holds the BERKELEY PATENT on that hat.

Todd: That's not the ISSUE. This EXTRAORDINARY SOJOURN is all for nothing because of some RALPH in a DERBY.

Phillip: Everything we've said has been picked up by ALUMINUM casements within the hat.

Todd: EXQUISITE.

Phillip: They've a SECRETARY setting down each and every word, transcribing it all for the queen.

Todd: I suppose there's some Sherlock Holmes type pretending that this cuffing is simply ELEMENTARY.

Phillip: No, I think there's BEEN the use of music CONSERVATORY students, an old school detective and his band of otters, a LABORATORY rat and the better part of thirty-two osteopaths.

Todd: The COMPENSATORY damages we can sue for, though, since we've done nothing.

Phillip: But the DYNASTY I wanted to build, the theatrical world I wanted to enter.

Todd: We can still SCHEDULE that in after we've appeared in court.

Phillip: I forgot to tell you that hope is not in our receiving a just sentence.

Scene of All Sounds Mixed Together

Crane: Congratulations, sir. The grotesque raft has been passed over the water, and shall burn into mere air.

Abercrombe: It was only possible because the otter talked the tenor into wearing that diaper, and the fur detecting wire within the otter's tail. They may sneer at our fair hearts, but darn it, we bore it, and we can now say that weve secured the longnose filefish.

Crane: And all they can now conspire to do is try to find a lawyer who will not cower when confronted with the hilarity of their case.

Abercrombe: They shall stew in their own juices, and shall be clad in stripes, be packed in little vans with whirring little lights, and they shall try to raffle rabbits to beat the habit of thanking us for our ruse.

Crane: The mound we've walked over to protect the ox, when we saw the body hot with the noise of high rhyme. What beef could they have with us now at the castle?

Abercrombe: Deep down, they know we are the ones to police this world, to have as protectors of pristine eels and prawns.

Crane: And if the tint of this tale becomes legendary, we shall see our people obey, to stop acting like rakes, to no longer be slaves to their tempers.

Abercrombe: And the pastor's blue boots, they were found by the garage façade in a supple cup of basted pork entrails. What organs pork have!

Crane: I am about to congratulate you again, sir. Good work, with every clue being doled out by that otter.

Abercrombe: Remember, I've know the triggerfish longer than anyone.

Crane: Let them rejoice then, too. For the exquisite solving of the most difficult case.

Abercrombe: And without the morning's toast, without the tenor's most lyrical epic to endure. I am ready to seek a shadow.

Epilogue

Stendahl: The bleeding gums of the aristocracy cannot be tamped with tissue paper anymore than the sockets of poets can be filled with glass. Let us not kick the genuine article when the false front can be abused in its place. The prayer for benevolence cannot be said in a church, for a power places the body into abject resignation. Stealth, I say, is the cup form which we drink. And the wine will glide past the tongue as though an organism that is transformed by more than glass, cork, oxygen and a hint of yeast. To the trenches go the poets, building little crystals from which the line resists its natural pause. Where might the fountain look for the gaze that harkens the shift that was neither by the bedside nor near the corpse. The voice, relentless in its commotion, bares down on my bones, but I didn't tell him. I turned instead to you, pouring myself a glass twice filled and slurp. Then to mangrove I go, seeking the rotting flesh of nobility run amok and poets blinded by their muse. Neither frightens the child, but that is not our first concern. Let time resist our eating of bananas when orchards are freshly poisoned. Watch the child grow fat on love and sweet lies, then hang yourself or run the steel through my ribs, either way, leave the deed answered. No small winners we, for we have drunk from the vine too often to be amazed, too rarely to be enraptured by the pit in our stomach's stomach. Shift in your seats, go on, but recall the warning when the blood begins to flow—the mouth caving in from lies and dexterity. Then pull out your own tongue, broil it for an hour, and walk slowly into the future. This may not work for all of us, but it does keep me from dangerous matters nearer by. The poets, for instance, feeling ever more frantic for a flower to feel, so that the eye of memory will not flag. But the flowers die, the mind's eye wilts, you say. But the poem, regardless, lives. And the hand resting on the throat is tranquil.

Disciplining Dimes

A Play by Gale Nelson

Dramatis Personae

Briggs
Sir
Stubbs
Lady Coo
Sharon
Sandra
Lucy
Alfredo
Octavio
Palidra
Aristotle

Scene / b /

Briggs: Your BIB sir.

Sir: Oh BOY! What's it going to BE, BROWN BROILED lamb BLENDED with HERBS?

Briggs: I amUNABLE to serve that FEEBLE dish once again, sir.

Sir: TUBES of BOURBON then, in a BOX of BLEACHED corn.

Briggs: BAD idea, sir.

Sir: I BOOKED this TABLE two weeks ago, so that I could IMBIBE on BABY lamb on a BED of OBSCENELY BRIGHT BASMATI rice. I would settle for a BALL of VEGETABLES, BRAISED with squid ink, BUT you must explain what is it going to BE?

Briggs: We have BOOKED an ABSOLUTE RUBE on which we anticipate your IMBIBING.

Sir: ABSURD!

Briggs: We have for your employment a MAMBO BAND led by the IBSEN LAB and BOB on OBOE. We know of your love of their song, "SUBZERO ORB."

Sir: It's lamb I love, not that BLIGHT of a BAND I tolerate.

155

Briggs: That's a BABE in a TUB BACK BEHIND the curtain, sir.

Sir: Are there any reporters around?

Briggs: None, sir.

Sir: Then I think I'll have a BOUT with my NIB, EBB and flow, you might say.

Briggs: We shall IMBUE you immediately.

Scene / k /
Stubbs: Those dimes are ATTACKING me again!

Lady Coo: My dear, that is a RISK of INACTION.

Stubbs: ASK them to PARK their portrits of F.D.R. before they IRK me further.

Lady Coo: WELCOME them into your heart, offer TALCUM powder rubs, CLOSE your fist around them as they lie on that table, QUIETLY.

Stubbs: What dimes!

Lady Coo: Dimes, indeed. The FACT is, I CAN only PICTURE them as you might a dog, a MURKY-headed wolfhound in need of discipline.

Stubbs: What I wouldn't give for well-disciplined dimes. They ATTACK the NUCLEAR family, the LACTOSE in mother's MILK, the treeless orchard of our COMMUNITY'S greatest OXYMORON!

Lady Coo: Enough of this SKIRTING of the issue. Bring me the dimes.

Stubb: COULDN'T you PICK them up?

Lady Coo: Bring me the dimes.

Stubbs: What a PICKLE. I've got to STICK my hand on that table with the dimes.

Lady Coo: Do it, slide them into a TOOLKIT, anything.

Stubbs: Those dimes are SCARY!

Lady Coo: A woman has to do everything, it seems.

Scene / d /
Sharon: I'm PLEASED to report that the DATE can be TODAY LODGED in the DEED as a CONDUIT to ORDER the DATA.

Sandra: Excellent.

Sharon: DID you know, no DOUBT you DID, that the EDICT EXPOSED our collaborators, but was BLIND to our own BIRD in the HAND?

Sandra: Excellent.

Sharon: They HAD OBSERVED the DEBT levels which PROVED the DRIVE SAGGED toward DOOM. We HAD the DIRT on them EXPOSED to save our own DOTTING of the 'i', so to speak.

Sandra: Excellent.

Sharon: The DIMES are in the BANDANA at the moment, PLEASED and in ORDER.

Sandra: DISCIPLINED?

Sharon: No such luck. They GORGED a DOG on the way over, RIGGED a gun AND AIMED it at my own HEAD. These DIMES are DANGEROUS, you can be sure of that, but we have FOUND a manner in which their EDGED pattern can be TURNED against them, for short PERIODS. TEETHED, they are, of course, CARED for, of course, but DUE to this, I am DOOMED to carrying them in a HEADDRESS or pieces of foul DRAPERY.

Sandra: I am PLEASED by this report. My DAUGHTER collects nickels, you know, and they TRIED to give her a DOSE of ODOR-free BIRD liver, which I SOLVED; as she DOZED, I took her on a DRIVE to the EDDY, SMILED at the nickels, and DINED on OLD pre-GUMMED apple pie. As the nickels SAGGED in my presence, they knew their plan was DOOMED. They MOUTHED their sorrow, I forgave, AND on we went, HAND in HAND to EDIT the tomb of ADAM out of the commemorative coins of EDEN.

Sharon: Excellent.

Sandra: As for the DIMES, DEAL with them. ADIEU.

Scene / t /
Lucy: TEA from a TIN?

Alfredo: ACT natural, as though THAT FATSO TWERP WEREN'T such a SOFT SIFTER.

Lucy: I can TASTE TATER TOTS BETWEEN my TEETH from LAST evening's sup.

Alfredo: The RESTROOM hoax, IT MUST be a TWIST on the TAX TOSS. STAY here, love.

Lucy: SIT down, Alfredo. You HAVEN'T the EATS.

Alfredo: Good idea. The TRAPEZE ARTIST MIGHT SUSPECT something if IT appears THAT I'm ready TO fast. SET a POT in FRONT of me.

Lucy: THAT'S BETTER. LET me TIE the bib on, so the STRING cheese WON'T muss your collar.

Alfredo: The TOWN ALTRUIST just walked in. TRY NOT TO STARE. Think of the TONE we MIGHT GET if he looked our way AT the wrong frequency.

Lucy: TEST the TOAST WON'T you?

Alfredo: Mmph. TACTILE, this TOAST is TACTILE. I THOUGHT IT was TOY TOAST!

Lucy: TOY TOAST indeed! The EASTERN figs, perhaps; the ASTROBEAN you TOOK for TROUT, yes. But TOAST?

Alfredo: He ITCHED! TWELVE TIMES, no less.

Lucy: Enriched WHITE bread, my love, or do you WANT another piece to TAX your TASTE buds thoroughly?

Alfredo: He OUGHT TO be carrying the LOOT, for the TRADE-off. But his TIGHTS expose his physique, not bundles of BOOTY.

Lucy: I ATE here LAST week with THAT ADROIT Mr. Rorsch, who could EAT like a horse. He would TASTE the dish and claim his GOUT was ACTING up. Then he would shiver, awfully.

Scene / f /

Sir: Briggs! I want my BILLFOLD.

Briggs: May I OFFER my condolences, to the SHEAF of papers you currently represent.

Sir: Yes, yes, FATHER of the country, all that FOG, best since TAFT, I've been told. But I won't SUFFER any longer without my BILLFOLD.

Briggs: It happens to be empty, sir.

Sir: My FATHER LEFT it FULL ENOUGH. I'm OFF to FIND the SAFE and FLUFF it back up.

Briggs: Then we look FORWARD to seeing you again soon, sir.

Sir: Only IF that AWFUL Bob is gone. Bring back the FLOTSAM Trio, they always made an EFFORT; they played FAST, made me LAUGH, got my FEET tapping.

Briggs: Over the FLAME, sir.

Sir: No IFS, buts or whens. The FATE of my GOLF game relies on your bringing back the FLOTSAMS. I'll be AFFABLE toward the whole establishment, as BEFITS my having been coming here my entire adult LIFE.

Briggs: The OAF lost his cello, sir.

Sir: Buy him a new one, FOR goodness sake. He could really play those F-MINOR passages.

Briggs: I've wrapped the lamb in FOIL.

Sir: I'll SIFT through the remains tonight, surely. No FEATHERS mixed in as a joke, I hope. No FOES of concertina music pickled in FOR my square jaw.

Briggs: On my word.

Scene / g /

Stubbs: Those dimes GIVE me the creeps!

Lady Coo: You and those VULGAR dimes. They ARGUE a GOOD GARGLE, but any GUY worth his GREEN hair would not GET BOGGED down in GAB about dimes.

Stubbs: That's just because you can't discipline them!

Lady Coo: The house ORGAN, once AGAIN playing GET the Lady Coo, GET the Lady Coo. You're in LEAGUE.

Stubbs: Coins, is it? The PENGUIN upstarts GROWL about GAWKING at GOD, and you're reduced to calling them coins!

Lady Coo: You GROUCH! You GLASSY-eyed, dime-pinching TAILGATE of an EGG, you think dimes are easy to deal with? Weeks, I tell you weeks. I'll GET those dimes in order but it takes weeks.

Stubbs: Ah, the UNGUENT smell of dimes after they've been under your tongue, something like GRUYERE cheese or GAUCHE little tablets of YOGURT.

Lady Coo: GET out of my experimental apartment complex!

Stubbs: You've GOT my dimes, AGLEAM with your upper lip's sweat. A GUY'S GOING to want them back, OLGA.

Lady Coo: Lady Coo, to you.

Stubbs: The SUGAR from your morning coffee adheres to the edges of the dimes once used in vending machines. The little larvae of the BUG you smashed on the dining room table, immediately excited the meld.

Lady Coo: I'll have you know that I am the GREATEST dime specialist in all of this region.

Stubbs: Yes, but you're still GOING about it the old way, one week at a time. One recalcitrant coin pulls you back to square one time and time AGAIN.

Lady Coo: You came to me, buster.

Scene / h /

Octavio: HE HIT me! I HATE this dime!

Palidra: HELLO, Octavio, I see you've HUNG your HAT right over the coin cortege.

Octavio: Those plastic figurines. HA HA HA. Cortege indeed.

Palidra: Well stop looking so HOT under your collar, come in out of the HALL, and squeeze me once or twice.

Octavio: I'll HOOK onto you any day. And for WHOM were you waiting downstairs, by the way?

Palidra: The society of numismatics were going to drop by to see my quarters.

Octavio: That's HIGH praise. Last week the AHOY group to look at your yoga photos, this week son to see the coins.

Palidra: HOW much time should I wait, do you think? They said they were going to come straight way, once they HAD HEALED the boy with the bicentennial penny collection, by singing HYMNS to HIS HAZED-over mother.

Octavio: We could HEAD into the sitting room surely, or HAS that room been shut down now too?

Palidra: HASPED, I'm afraid. The quarters are HOGGING all the downstairs rooms at this point. I HOVER HERE and there, HOPING to keep them from HIDING in the oak, lemon-lined drawers upstairs.

Octavio: What HAPPENED to your HOYLE?

Palidra: We never play card games in the HOUSE during the summer, too much HEAT.

Octavio: Is this his doing? I could HELP. I'd be more than HAPPY, for what HARM could be done by playing a few card games?

Palidra: HE says I HOB-nob with the wrong sorts. HOOF it up, HE suggests, dance with the HOOT and HIVE gang. I HOWLED at that counter-offer.

Scene / hw /

Aristotle: WHERE is it you'd rather be than here? WHAT would you be wearing? WHY? WHICH film holds your interest weeks after viewing? Did it OVERWHELM you with special effects, or dialogue? WHEN did you see it, early evening, midnight, or matinee? Did you ever WHACK the head of another patron of the cinema for hooting at the talents of an underachieving starlet? Or did you join in the WHIS-TLING? WHOA, I say, eat some carrots before answering these next few questions, for it is with some reluctance that I ask. Did the form of democracy taken by the Athenians WHET the WHEEL of justice or was the counter full of brochures for holidays in Turkey? Did the WHEAT embargo of the Nixon era bring to the knees the peasants of the East, or was it the WHELPS of little pigs brought to state fairs in Idaho? WHAT is behind the WHITENESS of the WHALE, and did Ahab live with all his faculties? WHAT WHARF can be found in New Bedford, and how many extra-toed cats are still in the vicinity? Take a long pause, and a WHIFF of WHIPPED cream, WHILE I consider the relative value of accepting a dime. WHIMPER with me, turn WHITE as they pretend to offer WHISKEY, WHICH I willingly drink knowing it, or thinking it, to be another liquid. I WHIRL around, drunk not with alcohol, and WHOOP. Therein lies my immortality. The last oblivious WHOOP.

Scene / ʤ /

Lucy: The GINGER PIGEON sounds lovely, dear.

Alfredo: This MESSAGE is URGENT. I must tap it under the table with this dime.

Lucy: Or should we try the GYPSY BLUEJAY, in GENTLE JAW-infused gravy?

Alfredo: If only I can get the dime out of my JEANS pocket. I've put on weight. They BULGE with my thighs. I'm JABBING at it but it won't move. I can't get out of the seat, too obvious. I'll have to NUDGE it up slowly.

Lucy: This must be a JOKE! JET-black GERBIL AGED in the JUICES of a hamster.

Alfredo: It's LODGED right there. Ow, I GOUGED myself. Oh, what a JOB I've got!

Lucy: You've gone all JOWLY, Alfredo. You must be famished. What a JOY, to come to this restaurant.

Alfredo: It's right at the EDGE of my BADGE, but it seems LODGED on the sharp star EDGE. Can I URGE it off?

Lucy: BARGE soup, honey! It sounds wonderful.

Alfredo: It's a GYP, love, a TANGIBLE first-rate GYP. Get the chicken soup with rice and hand me a dime.

Lucy: In GENERAL. I agree with your tastes, but BARGE soup. I would so love to try it, if only once.

Alfredo: Fine. Just hand over a dime.
Lucy: All I've got with me is the credit card, dear. Will that do?

Alfredo: Oh great ENGINE of trouble; this pair of JEANS, this dime LODGED on the EDGE of my BADGE, what would the LEIGE say, what would the boss say, what shall I say when the opportunity passes, and all I can do is say, pass the chicken soup, when I could have been dining on GERBIL?

Scene / I /

Sandra: You could at LEAST LIST the coinage projects, LEST we come into a ditching.

Sharon: I could LAY down the tracks for such projects DIRECTLY, you'd LAUGH how QUICKLY it'd get done. But I LACK the directive.

Sandra: EXCELLENT. I'LL LOCK you to your desk. I'LL LAY down the LAW. You LOAF and pretend it is SIMPLY the FOLLOWING of orders. Your SLOW, THISTLE-paced work FILLS my LIFE with an UNCURABLE ULCER, ALTHOUGH it could ALSO be the upshot of ALL that SLAW I've been eating.

Sharon: Not so LOUD! Think of your daughter's LOINS. She's in there with the ELECTRIC EEL, PROBABLY ringing our BELLS, UNWITTINGLY, TELLING ILL TALES of how we PAL around.

Sandra: A dime is over her head. She knows that if she TELLS the EEL anything, I'LL CURL her, SHE'LL PALL in my presence. I'LL HURL her across the room. I'LL stick dimes up her BLOUSE. Take away her PEARL earrings, run her up the FLAG POLE, INLAY her NICKELS with rust.

Sharon: EXCELLENT!

Sandra: I'LL CHANNEL ONLY the harshest sentiments to snap her ULNA, PULL it with an anger so LARGE, SHE'LL WAIL. My TOIL of FAMILIAL pressing SHALL COMPEL me to PLAY the ROLE so WHOLLY she would FLINCH, begin to become FLUSTERED, EMPLOY every entreaty known to her, CALL out OPENLY for HELP, GULP at my every motion, remove from her own mouth the PLAQUE- covered dentures that I bought for her LAST birthday, CLEAR her throat, and FLY.

Sharon: The POOL of BLOOD would be enormous.

Sandra: Any CLOWN would CLEARLY state. "She ALMOST swayed beneath that ELM, but salmon LEAP much higher."

Sharon: Where the OWL sits, yes, what a sight that would be. I SHALL hope the EEL hears nothing. It must be four O'CLOCK, she's been in there some great time.

Sandra: How the horizon begins to GLOW, with a GLINT of first rays making mirages of IGLOOS. LET us offer ALMS to the dimes, and then set down our coinage projects.

Scene / m /

Lady Coo: Oops. That SPASM in the heart of MY BOSOM caused ME to drop those DIMES.

Stubbs: You act as though a DAMSEL distressed, CALMED by a MIX of MALT in this MUG.

Lady Coo: Well, I tried to shuttle the recalcitrant DIME into the PRISM, but it IMPELLED ME to MOUTH the words of Shakespeare's DRAMA, "The ENAMEL BOMB."

Stubbs: That play was not by Shakespeare, M'LADY. It was a TERM paper of the EMCEE of the nightly lottery drawings. A Japanese No-style DRAMA, if I recall correctly, given on MATS woven with Shetland pony MANES and MOP ends FROM the MALL in Bath Spa. The lead actor had a MOLE, so under stage LAMPS her MOUTH suggested a MOIST MOOD not quite NORMAL. She REMINDED ME MOST frightfully of a DIME.

Lady Coo: Oh, you're right. I so like the ARM-chair scene with the face-wigged doctor, who took notes while she SCREAMED, "MA MA, MA MA."

Stubbs: Not Shakespeare at all.

Lady Coo: They were wearing tights, though. And the ALMS SEEMED SIMILAR—and the language SEEMED like so MANY GEMS skirting through the air, as though of the tongues of these gods and goddesses, so MANY RAMESE-like MEN, not a DIME-sucking SIMP AMONG THEM.

Stubbs: I do not suck DIMES either. I'm a LAMB-bone sucker, a LLAMA-bone sucker too, even one who EXHUMES the pit of a DAMSON to suck on but, really, Lady Coo, DIMES? They scare ME far too MUCH.

Lady Coo: I tried to SAMPLE one yesterday, but it bit MY FOREARM. Then it MADE an ATTEMPT to escape, by running down the block, rolling with a force known only by the gravity found near Wall Street.

Stubbs: Could you retreive it?

Lady Coo: It's been beneath my tongue, is there even now, as we speak.

Scene / n /

Octavio: I'm DOWN ON ONE KNEE, my Palidra, put DOWN your KNITTING AND allow me to cast a NET for your AFFECTIONS. NAME your ANTHEM, ANGEL.

Palidra: NAT says you're NOTHING but a DANDY, a DUNCE, but I like the way you DANCE.

Octavio: DON'T say NO, my love. DON'T GNAW at the KNOBS KNOWN to me as my KNEES. Be NICE AND make some lovely NOISE NOW. Say yes.

Palidra: LEAN IN closer, Octavio. ANOTHER TEN INCHES. ON my ANCIENT family's word of HONOR, you ENCHANT me. AN OUNCE of PINS AND NEEDLES are worthy of this MOMENT, AND a MONTH of UNHINGED flights of FANCY await our love.

Octavio: Say the word, my love.

Palidra: Yes, a HUNDRED times, yes. We shall walk to TOWN AND UNDO the PINS that hold up my hair ON the TENTH day of this coming MONTH to tell the world of our love.

Octavi: THEN CHANGE out of that FLANNEL NIGHTGOWN NOW, for we shall DANCE on the LAWN ON our OWN two sets of feet, CHANELLING our ENERGIES together.

Palidra: I must first look IN ON the quarters. The COINS, you KNOW, must always come first.

Octavio: Palidra, ON this NIGHT of all NIGHTS, the CHANGE that most CONSIDER bus fare shall come before the CHANGE IN our RELATIONSHIP? Before our first be-witched kiss?

Palidra: They are my ILLNESS.

Octavio: And you MINE. So put TINSEL IN our hair, and I shall FONDLE the dimes while you place SCENTED OINTMENTS ON the quarters.

Palidra: The dimes still bite, my sweet.

Octavio: Oh, so do I.

Scene / ŋ /

Sir: SING to me Briggs, get that blasted band to stop BANGING the GONG, and keep the stage cleared. Then SING to me.

Briggs: The TINGALING SINGER is coming shortly, sir, a far more impressive act than me.

Sir: He is from that YOUNG GANG of grouches. I don't want to hear him.

Briggs: Here presents the ANGER of ENGLAND, sir. And AMONG your own followers, he's begun to pick up steam.

Sir: I'll give him the FINGER.

Briggs: That could only lead to ANGUISH, sir. The photographers are here tonight, and the band is NEARING the end of its break, so I shall disappear again for some many minutes. Is there ANYTHING you'd like from the kitchen?

Sir: The squid-infused waffles, I think. Or perhaps the plate of unadorned cashews, maybe both dishes.

Briggs: And the sorcery-braised hamhocks?

Sir: Oh, do you have some of those?

Briggs: Our RINGER brought them just an hour ago.

Sir: That makes me salivate, most uncomplicatedly.

Briggs: Very good, sir.

Sir: But BRING the cashews, too. Wouldn't want to end the night without a cashew.

Briggs: I'll serve it from a non-GANGRENE-CAUSING ornament.

Sir: I applaud your resolute management!

Scene / p /

Aristotle: Did they PEEL the cashews for the clientele? Must the PILL be swallowed whole? We PAY the bill with a PET canary, or PAT the final bilge with PAPA-like fondness. Which is it to be? You need not answer all of these questions POST-haste, but don't sit on the POT when there's a line out to the lobby at the interval. Don't make them PAW their way through the second act, but when PLAYING cards, take the role of PONE when availed. I have nothing more to suggest, as I PINE for a POINT of view to take on the question of certainty. Oh hallowed unities! I have tried not to POUT about this distress but cannot SLEEP at night. They say my LIP has gone toward the TEPID recasting of the latest sophist's mumbo-jumbo into the easily digested coin of the realm. I do not APE one or another of these PASSING fancies, nor am I a mere amalgamation of Socrates and PLATO. I can LAP them on any field of philosophy, POP them with questions that once PUT into their PIPES, they'd have nothing but a PALPABLE smell, PULP. They think I PRIMP myself full of EPSOM salts, HARPY HAIRPINS and EARPLUGS cannot CARP me into retirement, not after what PLATO'S done for his REPUTATION—that SUPPLE turning of phrase set down to PAPER. Even Samuel PEPYS was known to SPLURGE by buying a new translation. So when looking for a Socratic argument, PLAY with dimes instead and let my POINT of view come through. I was not the first, most surely, but I know the sound mines makes is better than most. And I can SPLIT hairs with the very best.

Scene / s /

Lucy: SIT down, my Alfredo

Alfredo: I SEE you've already ordered. What do you SAY, shall we ALSO get SOME SAKI?

Lucy: I GUESS a little SAUCE might be NICE. I SAW they had CAT'S SQUAB as a SPECIAL, one of LIFE'S greater pleasures. So I ordered it in a SOY SAUCE.

Alfredo: Or should we have SOME Dry SACK? That SETS my nerves to REST. Damn, the acrobat is here. We'll have to keep our VOICES down, and I can't afford to get TIPSY.

Lucy: They don't use paper bags or foil here to prepare the SQUAB, but rather athletic SOCKS. I think it is quite the perfect way to make the bird rich with SAUCE, and yet meek in AFTERTASTE. A STONE from the SOUTH SQUARE TOPSOIL holds the SOCK closed, rather than one of those terrible pink clothes pins they used to use.

Alfredo: I GUESS I can tap out the codes while she TALKS of food. If only I'd remembered that BLASTED dime!

Lucy: I MISS not having the CALF'S liver in MOUSE dung and mushroom CAPS, but they tell me the liver touched ICE THIS morning.

Alfredo: I'll OFFSET THIS LOSS by blinking my MESSAGE to the MESMERIST.

Lucy: They tell me that the OATS they use are actually here on LEASE from the ESQUIRE ACROSS the STREET, SO I demurred.

Alfredo: A little more VERBOSE, my dear. I'm trying to PASS the word without the help of a dime.

Lucy: Are you letting our CONVERSATION go ASTRAY SIMPLY SO you can clear your head? What blinking! PERHAPS you need a new PRESCRIPTION. That much blinking SUGGESTS that SOMETHING MUST be wrong.

Alfredo: YES, YOUTH'S DEATHS, the plans in BOOTS, the manner in which we MYSTIFY the Penny Brigade ONCE more, all SAUCE for the GOOSE, in a manner of SPEAKING. IFS pile up, one at a time. Dimes by the dollar.

Scene / ʃ /

Sharon: The OFFSHOOT is that SHE can SHAKE the OCEAN FISSURE with her TISSUE MACHINE, SHOULD SHE get the nickels to conform to her desires.

Sandra: That would USHER in chaos.

Sharon: Most SURELY. SHE has come upon a way to CUSHION the SHOUTS of the quarters that have been used to gear the nickels properly. But the SHELL in which SHE wants the nickels to place themselves is still too ASHEN for them to comply. But SHE may succeed soon.

Sandra: Let's substitute my daughter's nickels for hers. We'll send her down the SHAFT with them. SHE'S SHY but SHE'LL do it for us.

Sharon: Her nickels? Didn't they try to kill her with livers? They are as undisciplined as dimes.

Sandra: Don't be silly, SHARON. They are still wild nickels. They are as undisciplined as dimes.

Sharon: You're SURE? They aren't WISHY-WASHY sometimes?

Sandra: Never. My daughter is in constant danger, with them around. Now, let us SHOUT for her to join us. I'll get the heavy-duty crab-leg SHAWL and SHAKE it out while you get my daughter.

Sharon: SHE has a deep SHIN bruise. Perhaps we ought to offer the penny-coated knee pads, too. We could SHOW her how we wore them on the SHILLING caper in Austria.

Sandra: Good idea. We couldn't save the SHAH, but we did acquire some well-behaved SHILLINGS. Why don't we mix some of them in with the nickels?

Sharon: That would raise SUSPICIONS.

Sandra: You're right.

Scene / θ /

Palidra: We must BOTH take our OATH while we walk along a SOUTH-facing PATH.

Octavio: THROUGH THICK and THIN, our EARTH warrants we come upon a HEARTH, to declare our love to brethren, mostly yours.

Palidra: THUMB rings, I THINK, would be a customary gift for family members. And some MONTHS later, my sister shall declare her FIFTH BIRTH complete, on a rock near sweet BATH water.

Octavio: THANK goodness for HEALTH in your sister's body. THROUGH and THROUGH she has no WRATH, distress. She is ready again to BIRTH a child.

Palidra: HEALTHY, she is ENTHRALLED BOTH by our wedding and her approaching day.

Octavio: Will she use ETHER again?

Palidra: No, instead a SOOTH has suggested she should spell PITHY puns WITH her big left toe on a HEARTH, and a MOTH on her lips.

Octavio: I hope we are back from our ETHOS, PATHOS and BATHOS THEATER tour before she delivers.

Palidra: What luck, to attend a full cycle of Greek tragedies on our honeymoon.

Octavio: WITH promised THUNDER storms on Crete!

Palidra: I THANK heaven for our happiness.

Octavio: And to realize we are going to pay for our wonderful trip WITH proceeds from your yoga photos.

Palidra: Well, I couldn't part with any of my quarters.

Scene / ð /

Aristotle: THE SMOOTH aspect of abstraction need not be intertwined so THAT THOSE who prefer mimesis untrammelled can enjoy THEIR fare. ALTHOUGH we feel THE two are SMOTHERING one ANOTHER, BOTHER not THIS delineation THUSLY. RATHER, come closer, play so close to reality THAT TITHES are offered by my noble theories. BATHE yourself in ideas, THEN come to THE setting to have your sweating brow SOOTHED. TETHER THE actors' MOUTHS, give reasons more frequent THAN THOSE of THE least reviewing critic for THE closing down of all idiocy, such as THIS coming before you, and cram into THE framework known most sorely as THE realistic play, where palsy can be played for a sympathetic two hours or more, where THOSE with bleeding ulcers cringe with unsightly precision and love-sick couples are a dime a dozen. THE world itself is bled dry without some modern forces. Am I critic of my own ideas, or is it merely a question of centuries passing translations by? Some stubborn sorts are unwilling to contemporize THEIR minds—I say leave THEM to THEIR THEES and THOUS and OTHER patrons long outdated. Give to me a season pass to what I know so well—THE entire sweep of stage history's time, all of it alive, in context.

Scene / ʌ /

Lucy: If EVER I HAVE to spend the night alone, how much JAVA would I pour down my neck?

Alfredo: VICTORY, I feel ENLIVENED by the VIVID feel of being INVINCIBLE, no longer VICTIM to tight jeans, but gaining VENGENCE for those VENOMOUS past VISITS.

Lucy: Answer me, dear, how much coffee would I drink were you not here by my side?

Alfredo: A pot, LOVE, my Lucy, dear. A pot of VICE-strewn VULGAR mud. I

MARVEL at how you SWIVEL in your chair, chain-drinking.

Lucy: And I feel EVER so much that we share so much VICTUAL history with VERVE, in this establishment.

Alfredo: The TWELVE ELVES are coming in through the EAVES. A VIOLENT VALOR is necessary. ABOVE them the VULTURES of state, rolling like so many eggs gone green, making roof-top noise as though reindeer HOOVES, PROVING all Christmas myths, coincidentally.

Lucy: How dreadful! Come take COVER under the table with me.

Alfredo: Damn. I left the dime on top of the table. And I can hear the dreaded FLIVVER SWERVING into the CURVE some half-mile up.

Lucy: And our VICHYSSOISE is beginning to warm up. It'll be no good by the time this VILE scene plays out.

Alfredo: I LOVE you, Lucy. HOW'VE we gone so long without a kiss? ENLIVEN my death!

Lucy: But can't you see the signs of a DOVE? I'VE been tapping nickels through it all.

Scene / j /
Sharon: YOU have got to stop feeding the YAK the JUNGIAN donuts.

Sandra: They are the best YELLOW pastries, though.

Sharon: But having retrieved the YAM-shaped helmet we gave YOUR own daughter to wear when we sent her to her demise should help YOU YIELD YOUR passion for feeding the YAK.

Sandra: This YOUNG daughter of mine, so YOKED to the ways of our own YOUTH-FUL flights of fancy, given a thorough YANK by that woman YESTERDAY!

Sharon: Most sad, surely.

Sandra: All I'm left with is a stack of worthless nickels!

Sharon: YES, Sandra. And the YAM-shaped helmet, a tub of egg YOLKS, and memories of her five favorite flavors of YOGURT.

Sandra: Her DYING words, which we could hear come up the chute so clearly shall always haunt me: "YIKES, YOUCH, my nickels, my wonderful nickels."

Sharon: Were it not for the passing YACHT, we surely would have been done in, too. And all we can do is talk of YET another caper gone bad. We must place less attention on the manner in which we get coins to do our dirty work, this I think, most fully.

Sandra: Daughters, too. YESTERDAY holds a bitter cast. And these nickels are my legacy's legacy. So let me not spend them fruitlessly on a garden of lettuce for the YAK. Let me keep them, so long as they live, in a bank with a mechanical apparatus.

Sharon: A true sign of YOUR deepest sorrow.

Scene / z /

Palidra: Shall we play JAZZ during the VOWS?

Octavio: I don't want to seem BLASE, but I would prefer HYMNS.

Palidra: That would FIZZLE out. WHOSE snappy BANGS of ZEAL would provide the right cover for SISTER'S SPASMS, should she have them, better than THOSE of a JAZZ band?

Octavio: With EASE, the ENZYME PRISMS could create BRIDGES from Gregorian Chants to Cole Porter TUNES. Belinda SINGS with them now, AS you know, and LONGS to be part of our SERVICES. She said she'd have her BANGS trimmed the week before.

Palidra: But would she cover over the six different ORANGES she'd dyed them? And IS it really WISE to have your old BUSINESS partner take part in our ceremony?

Octavio: She would go into a TIZZY if she can't take part.

Palidra: And I if she DOES.

Octavio: This planning BUSINESS ISN'T EASY, IS it?

Palidra: Not so long AS I want A and you want ZED. Let's EASE back into agreement. We'll have the Lady HENS BUZZ around the backyard, followed by the OMNICONS who can ZIP through a few fusion TUNES, then the ceremony proper. Your ENZYMS PRISMS can sing later on, once the cake's been cut, and I can dance so close to your ear.

Octavio: The ceremony IS once again YOURS to plan, and mine to have great hopes for.

Palidra: The QUARTERS have worked up a little skit for the rehearsal dinner.

Scene / ʒ /

Sir: I want this to be a CASUAL affair, but a VISION of great joy.

Briggs: A rehearsal dinner is just such an event that should always be MEASURED in how much ILLUSION of feast can be imparted.

Sir: These two are inseparable.

Briggs: And they should TREASURE their many days together.

Sir: I quite agree. I am sending them to the Azores when they get back from their honeymoon cruise, a LEISURE trip around the Classical Islands, so I'm told. Paid for by my daughter's artistic prowess in sitting, I'm proud to say.

Briggs: A PLEASURE, I'm sure, sir.

Sir: I told them that a marraige should not resemble a MIRAGE. For the closer one gets, the better the VISUAL landscape should become.

Briggs: Very good, sir. Now, what shall we serve?

Sir: Boxes of oysters, I think. And a xanthicles house wine. Perhaps a possum-filling cake with chocolate and octupus layers, and that poached AZURE salmon you never seem to serve me anymore.

Briggs: And the lamb?

Sir: Of course, the lamb! The lamb is to kill for!

Briggs: We think of it as garbage, no imagination involved in the preparation. But we shall be happy to serve it as though it were a TREASURE.

Sir: What more could I ask?

Scene / tʃ /
Stubbs: That dime just bit me. Naughty dime!

Lady Coo: I've been playing CHESS with that dime all week, and it would CHOOSE to CHEAT at every turn. WHICH reminds me, you haven't paid for my service yet.

Stubbs: BENCH that dime, first. It wanted to CRUNCH on my fingers.

Lady Coo: I'm no WENCH who can be spoken to as though I were a CHILD.

Stubbs: But the dime, it hurt me. It thought of me as BRUNCH.

Lady Coo: If you hadn't put your fingers into that bowl of CHERRIES, it may have left you alone.

Stubbs: That was KETCHUP, I was eating FRENCH fries for LUNCH.

Lady Coo: That accounts for the STENCH. What a CHOICE, KETCHUP on FRENCH fries indeed. Haven't you ever heard of CHUTNEY.

Stubbs: I couldn't CATCH that?

Lady Coo: I've a HUNCH you could, you WRETCH. Now, about these dimes. I was able to ETCH a little 'H' into EACH one, so that they are now magnetically repulsed by EACH other. The CHIPS of dime dust were collected in a small bowl and sent to the laboratory, where, under a powerful microscope, it was learned that someone STITCHED musical notations into their genetic codes. They hope to cross-breed these dimes with some wayward quarters I sent to the center last year. I dare say, I doubt the quarters will CATCH on to anything but three-four time very easily, but the dimes will do the leading.

Stubbs: Go on. I'm going to eat the rest of my CHOW.

Lady Coo: The dimes are unrepentant and cannot be CHIDED. They must be given free roam, preferably in a large, unfenced area. I would recommend sending them to WICHITA for the holidays this year, and see how a little distance from their normal environment affects them. If they are still dangerous, build a TRENCH, and know at all times which side they are on. These words were CHOSEN carefully. Will you follow them?

Stubbs: With a sadness that could be heard in the soul of a kitten.

Sources

Black, John W. & Irwin, Ruth B. *Voice and Diction*. Columbus, Ohio: C.E. Merrill, 1969.

Blunt, Jerry. *Stage Dialects*. San Francisco: Chandler Publishing Co., 1967.

Chopra, Dr. Depak. *Quantum Healing,* New York: Bantam, 1990.

Fairbanks, Grand. *Voice and Articulation Drillbook, 2nd Edition,* New York: Harper & Row, 1960.

Hahn, Elise etal. *Basic Voice Training for Speech*. New York: McGraw Hill, 1957.

Hendrickson, Robert. *American Talk*. New York: Viking, 1986.

Jones, Daniel. *An English Pronouncing Dictionary*. New York: Dutton, 1943.

Kenyon & Knott. *A Pronouncing Dictionary of American English*. Springfield, Massachusetts: Merriam, 1953.

Kokeritz, Helge. *Shakespeare's Pronunciationa*. New Haven, Connecticut: Yale University Press, 1953.

Martin, Howard R. *Analysis of the Dramatic Speaking Voice, A Practical System and Methodology*. Dissertation, University of Michigan, 1977.

O'Neill, Eugene. *Complete Plays*. New York: The Library of America, 1988.

Prator, Clifford H. & Robinett, Betty Wallace. *Manual of American English Pronunciation*. New York: Holt Rinehart, 1985.

Skinner, Edith. *Speak With Distinction*. New York: Applause Books, 1992.

"U.S. Census Report." *USA Today*. April 28, 1993.

Wells, J.C. *Accents of English*. Cambridge, England: Cambridge University Press, 1982.

Williams, Raymond. *The Long Revolution*. London, Chatto & Windus, 1961.